Oh, Boy! Babies!

Oh, Boy! Babies!

by Alison Cragin Herzig

and Jane Lawrence Mali

Photographs by Katrina Thomas

Little, Brown and Company

BOSTON   TORONTO

Also by Alison Cragin Herzig and Jane Lawrence Mali

A WORD TO THE WISE

FIRST EDITION

Library of Congress Cataloging in Publication Data

Herzig, Alison Cragin and Jane Lawrence Mali.
  Oh, boy! Babies!

  SUMMARY: A photo essay of a class in infant care given to fifth and sixth grade boys with the help of mothers and real babies.
    1. Baby sitters — Juvenile literature. 2. Infants — Care and hygiene — Juvenile literature. [1. Baby sitters. 2. Babies — Care and hygiene] I. Mali, Jane Lawrence, joint author. II. Thomas, Katrina. III. Title.
HQ769.5.H47   649'.1   80-16575
ISBN 0-316-35896-7
ISBN 0-316-35897-5 (pbk.)

H

Published simultaneously in Canada
by Little, Brown & Company (Canada) Limited

PRINTED IN THE UNITED STATES OF AMERICA

For our friend,
Mary Lee McGrath,
who never stopped opening doors.

The names of the boys in this book have been changed and the time span condensed. On occasion, minor editing of syntax and character composites seemed necessary in the interest of clarity and narrative cohesion. In all other respects, the story that follows is true.

Oh, Boy! Babies!

To Whom It May Concern:

   This is to certify that
has completed successfully a course in baby
care offered here at the school to grades V
and VI. Using actual infants, each student
learned to bathe, dress, feed, diaper and
handle a baby. In addition, we discussed the
other responsibilities required of a baby-
sitter: coping with emergencies, tidiness,
taking messages, among other duties.
   Each boy was also required to demonstrate
warmth, patience, common sense and good
humor. That   has received this
letter indicates that in all respects he has
my enthusiastic and wholehearted recom-
mendation.

                    Sincerely,

   Head of the Infant Care Course

2

Introduction

On A CERTAIN DAY in September of 1978, inside one of the thousands of schools across this country, something began. It began in assembly.

The school in question stands, as it has for more than two centuries, a few steps from a busy urban intersection and is entered through a crayon-red door. Once, long ago, it was small and coeducational. Now it is medium sized and for boys only.

On this particular morning Mr. Jacob, the principal, rose to make an announcement to the fifth and sixth grades. The announcement concerned the electives program for the fall term. Electives, a recent innovation at this school, are best described as mini-courses outside the normal academic program, and they are taught by volunteers — parents, teachers, and recruits from the community. Electives are for fun. They are also required. This appears to be a contradiction in terms, but then education is full of quirks and surprises. At this school a boy cannot choose not to choose an elective. He can, however, enrich his life with mechanical drawing, wall murals and other art forms, backgammon or croquet, kite flying, karate, photography, and computers, to name a few. The list is long. There is even a course on stand-up comedy, referred to by the boys as "The Funny Man."

The announcement is normally routine, but on this occasion Mr. Jacob proceeded with unaccustomed caution. He was skeptical about part of what he had to say. As far as he knew, it had never been said to a group of young boys before, and he wanted to slip it in and get it across without giving it an undue importance. Timing and tone were crucial. Therefore, it was near the middle of his prepared remarks, right after croquet, to be exact, that he announced in what he hoped was a noncommittal drone and simple, straightforward terms, "And next we are offering something new — an infant care class."

Having plunged, he kept going. "The course will cover six weeks, meeting every Wednesday afternoon," he explained, "and will be taught with the help of mothers and real babies. The participants will learn to bathe, dress, feed, diaper, play with, and handle infants. Coping with emergencies will be stressed, and each boy is expected to demonstrate warmth, patience, common sense, and good humor." He thought it wise to include the following incentive: "Boys who complete this course will receive an official certificate. They may use this to certify demonstrated confidence" — his words were getting bigger as he went along — "and possibly to request a raise in the fees or remuneration which they may charge as baby-sitters. As the class will be limited to ten students, I encourage you to put it high on your list of alternatives. I wish they had had a course like this when I was your age," he added. "A most interesting one, as I'm sure you will agree."

Agreement was not immediately apparent.

"You mean we're actually going to learn how to diaper a baby?" asked one ten year old.

"Yes," answered Mr. Jacob.

"Before? Or after?" asked the boy.

"After, of course."

"Oh, yuck!"

Later, in the sixth-grade classroom, another boy said loudly, "It's silly! They'll probably just use dolls."

"Besides, it's only a one-shot deal," added someone else. "We'll never get another chance with babies — in real life."

"Girls' stuff," said a third. "Who in his right mind would take 'Babies'?"

Nobody answered, but five of his classmates and five fifth graders listed it without consulting each other or telling a soul. There were enough boys and more than enough babies, so the class began as scheduled on the first Wednesday in October. That day it poured rain, but babies came anyway, in a front pack, a stroller, and a carriage. While there was nothing un-usual about babies in the lobby, when they kept going down the narrow corridor toward the stairs, boys hesitated and then cleared a path by flattening themselves against the walls. The varsity soccer team on the way to practice in numbered jerseys and knee sox stopped and peered into the carriage. Two of the players were recruited to carry it to the second floor. The rest of the team gaped up the stairwell as the carriage, maneuvered by their friends, rose slowly, rounded the landing, and dis-appeared from sight.

The First Wednesday

The baby class was something that everyone wanted, more or less, no matter what they said. But it was something you wouldn't talk about, at least not before you got it. You'd keep it to yourself. I could have cheated and beaten their system. We all know how to do that with electives, you know — put your first choice third and your third choice first and you fool them every time, if you follow me. But I didn't feel like doing it with "Babies." I wanted it from beginning to end. And I put it first. And I got it.
— *Rick*

I was never scared about the babies. I was just really happy.
— *Dylan*

I was a bit nervous at the beginning. I mean, a strange woman gives me her baby and I say, "Wait a minute! Aren't you going to teach me? I don't know anything yet." The baby thinks, maybe, "Oh, I'm perfectly safe with this boy," but I'm the one who's responsible. It's like you're teaching a new human being tricks and developing someone else's skills. It's a challenge. It's fun, but it's a challenge.
— *Seth*

I said, "Hooray!" I wanted to have a new experience, have an adventure, meet babies. I wanted to teach my older sister. She baby-sits. I thought I could give her some pointers.
— *Forrest*

If you drop 'em, you're dead.
— *Joey*

IN A ROOM on the second floor, the boys waited, sitting on the tops of desks, their legs dangling. The babies were late.

"Where are they?" asked Rick. He checked his digital watch with the moon-sized face and wide strap.

"Who's coming? What babies?"

"How old?"

"How many?"

"Are you sure they're going to be real live babies?" asked Smith.

"Well, I know why they're having this elective," said Luke. He tossed the hair back from his eyes. "Too many of the teachers are absent because they're having babies, so finally they just said, 'Bring 'em in!'"

"My mom's going to have a baby, too," said Joey.

"Where are they going to put them?" asked Dylan. "There's no room."

The boys looked around. All the chairs were piled with books and binders, and the carpeted floor between the rows of desks was littered with papers and scraps, baseball gloves, cleats, and sweats.

"This rug is unsterile," said Seth. He pulled at the knot of his necktie.

Forrest came through the door carrying a bulky white bundle. It looked like laundry.

"You're late. The class has begun," Luke told him.

"I got the mats. For the babies," said Forrest. "We're supposed to spread them, and Mr. Jacob said to move the desks back."

When the desks and chairs were lined against the walls, the floor looked worse than before. The boys picked up most of the scraps and kicked the rest of the junk out of the way. Then they began to unfold the mats.

"Spread them on the clean side," said Luke.

"Wait! The other side is cleaner," said Seth.

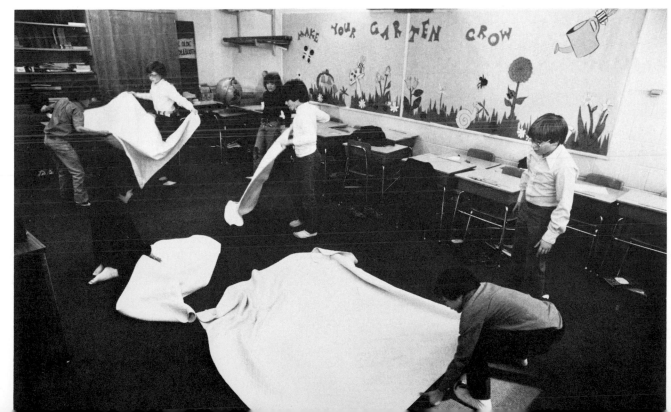

"I'm going to wash my hands," said Michael. Dylan went with him to the sink in the corner and they scrubbed up together.

"I gotta comb my hair," Forrest said.

"Oh, Forrest, you don't have to be that formal," said Seth.

"Talk about formal. What's with the necktie?" asked Luke. He and Seth had hold of opposite sides of one of the two large mats. Luke pulled. "Stop yanking, Seth. You're just making more wrinkles," he said.

"Do we have to take off our shoes?" asked Douglas.

"If you want to walk on the mats, you do," Forrest told him.

Rick had already removed his sneakers and stashed them out of reach on the counter by the sink. He padded around in his socks.

"Oh, Forrest, don't take off *your* shoes," he said.

"No. It's, 'Oh, Forrest, don't lift up your *arms*,'" said Luke.

"His shoes smell more. And don't leave them there. A baby might eat them," advised Rick.

"Rick and I can be in charge of this mat," said Luke.

"I'll operate with you, Forrest. Okay?" said Joey. With the four mats down, the room seemed ready for something.

"Maybe I better take off my watch before a baby swallows it. Or wees on it. I don't want my watch to turn yellow," said Rick.

"I thought there was a force field around it," said Smith.

"I'll tell you one thing I know about babies. If they're too young, they cry at everything. You tickle them and they whine," observed Douglas.

"I like babies. My mom's brother's wife's sister had a baby, so I know," said Forrest.

"My mom's going to have a baby, too," said Joey again. "I thought I should take this class. I need some pointers. There's nobody in my family younger than me."

"Will she bring it in?" asked Gordon. "When it's born, I mean."

"Sure. That's a great idea! I'll ask her."

"I've always wanted to baby-sit," said Dylan. "But I thought it would be better if I knew what I was doing."

"I don't have any brothers or sisters," said Michael, "but I go to the playground a lot to check out the babies."

The boys arranged themselves around the perimeters of the mats.

"Now what?" asked Smith.

"Wait," said Luke.

Quiet reigned for a few moments. Then Douglas dove at Forrest's waist, and the large center mat became a wrestling ring full of squirming, grunting boys.

"Shut up! I hear a baby," yelled Rick. He ran to the door. "Yup. The procession of babies."

"Charge!" said Luke.

Douglas had Forrest pinned. "Are they really coming? Really?" asked Forrest, trying to wriggle free.

"They're really coming," said Rick.

"Quick! Get off the mats," ordered Luke. "We're dirtying them for the kids. And remember, you guys, act *calmly!*"

"Look! Here they come! Number-one baby. Number-two baby," announced Rick.

"Oh, boy! Babies!"

"Hi, he, she, it, whatever," Rick greeted a baby in a carriage.

"Babies. Yummy!" said Luke.

"Is it a boy or a girl?" asked Rick.

"Girl," said Seth. "Her eyelashes are long. And she has a skirt on."

"Hi, everybody," said the young woman with the carriage. "This is Caroline. I'm her mother, Mrs. Maher, and I'm also the teacher."

Caroline was eight months old. She sat in the carriage with a pink-and-white-checked pillow in her lap. Rick pushed the carriage into the room and Forrest walked along beside it, his hands on the frame. Mrs. Maher followed them in. Strapped

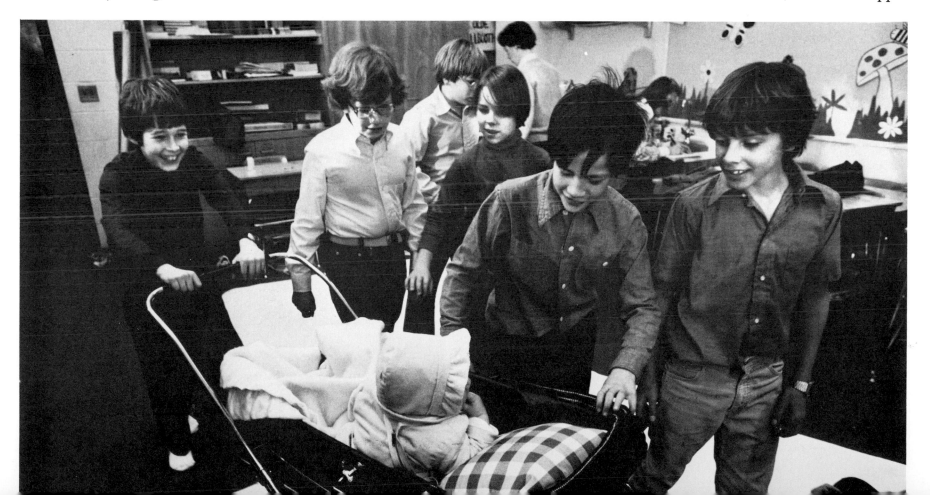

to her shoulders and suspended across her chest was a dark blue pouch. The pouch contained Henry. He was five months old. Henry was borrowed for the day.

"Where's his mother? Why would she let a five month old come out alone?" asked Joey.

"It's okay," said Forrest softly. "I'll take care of him."

"We'll take Caroline," said Seth. "She's cute."

Mrs. Maher picked Caroline out of her carriage and sat her in the middle of the center mat. Caroline looked uncertainly from one boy to another. Mrs. Maher laid Henry on another mat, the small one in front of the teacher's desk.

"Any more babies coming?" asked Michael.

"I think you'll only see these two today because of the rain," answered Mrs. Maher. "Now, this class is about taking care of babies and all the things . . ."

"Oh, no! Here comes another!" yelled Rick.

"Boys! Boys! Sssh." Mrs. Maher put a finger to her lips. "Let's keep a low, low tone. Loud noises and strange faces are frightening to babies. To anyone, for that matter."

Frederick arrived in a stroller.

"He's fourteen months old," said Mrs. Maher. "A heavy dude."

"A wide receiver or a defensive guard," decided Luke. "Look at him yawn. He's the champion yawner of the world."

"Okay. Look at these babies for a minute," said Mrs. Maher. "As you can see, there is an enormous difference between them, even though they are only a few months apart in age.

For example, it won't take you long to find out that Freddy can walk, Caroline can crawl, but Henry just sort of lies around. Why don't you start by taking off their jackets and hats and sweaters. Quietly and slowly."

"But Caroline's crying," said Joey.

"She's been fussy for the last few days. If you really want to know the truth, it's driving me bananas," said Mrs. Maher. "She may be coming down with a cold or cutting a tooth. Or what else do you think it could be?"

"She hurts?"

"Hungry?"

"Thirsty?"

"Tired?"

"She might have gone to the bathroom."

"Maybe she's shy," said Dylan.

Freddy's mother took him out of his stroller and stood him on the other big mat near the door. Freddy wouldn't sit down. He snuffled. Then he gave a long groan. Tears rolled down his cheeks. Michael looked around for help.

"Hey, boys," said Mrs. Maher. "It's not unusual for babies to cry. It can get boring and exasperating when you're baby-sitting, especially when they cry all the time. But don't take it personally and don't give up. Okay? Instead, comfort them. Pick them up. Hold them, cuddle them, whisper to them. They like that. Who'd like to learn how to pick up a baby?"

Hands rose all over the room.

"Me."

"I will."

"I said first."

"I'm afraid to," said Joey.

"There's no need to be," said Mrs. Maher. "To pick up a baby like Caroline you hook your hands under her arms, thumbs forward." She lifted Caroline up in the air as she spoke and held her there. Caroline wriggled and writhed. Her legs flailed, but she couldn't go anywhere. "See? Just be absolutely sure you have a good grip."

"Is there any difference between lefties and righties?" asked Forrest.

Mrs. Maher looked puzzled. "Ah . . . whatever is comfortable for you," she said finally. Then she put Caroline down and turned to Henry. "Now with infants like Henry, one hand goes under the fanny and one hand behind the head, like this. Here we go, Henry. And then you lift them up and settle them against your shoulder. The neck is the most important. It must be supported. At all times. Do you know why?"

"To keep their neck from whiplash?" suggested Joey.

"Right. Why don't you try picking up Henry now," Mrs. Maher said to him.

"Me?"

"Yes."

Joey studied the situation. He looked at Henry and then at Mrs. Maher and then back to Henry. Then he reached down, got a good grip, and began to lift very slowly.

"Higher, Joey. Higher," said Forrest.

"Hey, the neck! The neck!" warned Seth. "Put one hand behind his head."

Henry was up.

"You look nice with that baby," said Luke. "The perfect pair."

Joey navigated gingerly once around the room with Henry while Seth, Luke, and Forrest waited for their turn.

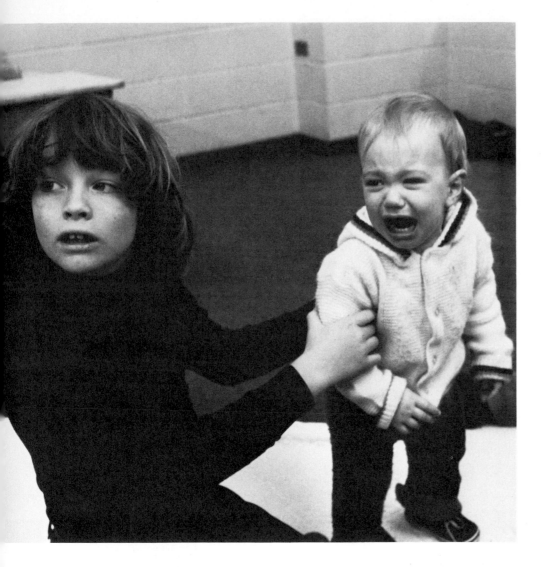

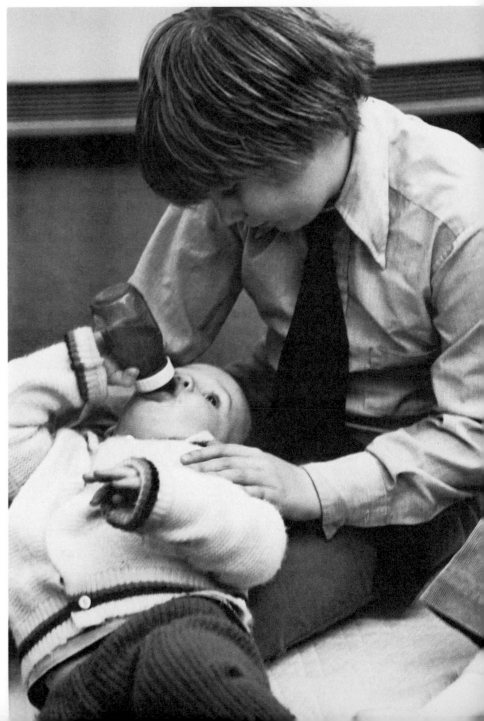

Michael and Smith tried to comfort Freddy. They stroked his head and showed him a book with pictures, but his groans grew longer. Finally Freddy's mother sent Seth over with a bottle of juice. Freddy grabbed for it.

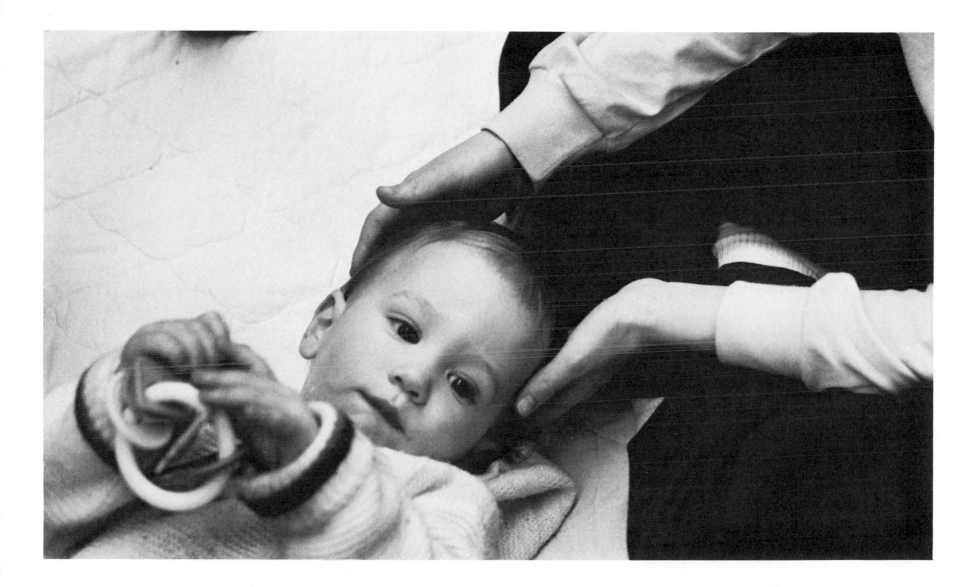

Meanwhile, Caroline was crying, too. She sat on the big mat in the middle of the room, wailing.

"I always think, how can babies make so much noise out of their teeny, weeny throats?" said Rick above the clamor.

"I know, let her look in this mirror," said Gordon. "She'll think it's a friend."

"And here's your doll, too," Dylan said softly.

"Do babies like music?" Rick wondered. "I could sing. 'The first Noel, the angels did say . . .' I guess not. But it used to work for my mom."

"If she's ticklish, that might make her stop," said Gordon.

"Her feet aren't. I've already tried," said Rick.

"Look at her hands. Tiny little hands." Dylan compared his hand to Caroline's. "Look at that. Look at how small it is. And jeez, look at her pinky nail!"

"She's turning red. Somebody do something. Pick her up, Dylan," said Rick.

"Mrs. ah? Mrs. . . . ah . . . Caroline's mother? To pick her up do I put my hands under her arms?"

"Yes," said Mrs. Maher. "Thumbs in front."

"Her thumbs?"

"No. Yours."

Dylan knelt down and hooked his hands under Caroline's arms. His fingers were stiff and his thumbs stuck forward. He heaved once and raised her a few inches off the mat.

"Keep going. Keep going."

But Dylan set Caroline back down, readjusted his grip, and

tried again. This time he made it. Caroline's teary face appeared over his shoulder. Dylan struggled to his feet.

"Jeez, Caroline, you gotta lose some weight," he said, sidestepping around Freddy. Caroline sobbed. "Want to see the sights out the window?"

Behind his back Rick made grinning faces at Caroline. "Hooray! She's stopped crying!" he shouted. "Look at her. She's laughing. She can laugh!"

"Rick. Your voice is too loud," cautioned Mrs. Maher. "I can hear it above everyone else's."

"Look at old Frederick, sitting back in his easy chair with a good drink," said Smith.

Frederick was slumped against Seth's knee, bottle in hand.

"He's satisfied. Finally," said Michael. "Are you satisfied, Freddy?"

"I think he just wet my leg," said Seth, "but I don't dare move."

"Your back must be killing you," Mrs. Maher said. "Oh, that's my fault. I should have told you that when you're giving a bottle, it's important that you be as comfortable as the baby, because if you're tense, the baby can feel it. There are no armchairs in this room, so you might try sitting against a wall next time."

Mrs. Maher handed Caroline's afternoon bottle to Gordon. Forrest walked bent legged around the room carrying Henry.

"Hey, Rick, want to have a turn with this one?" he asked as he passed the window.

"I smell something strange," said Rick. He sniffed at Henry. "Better get him checked."

Slowly and carefully Forrest lowered Henry onto the small mat. Henry lay flat, staring at the ceiling. Michael and Douglas crawled over to have a look at him.

"How you doing, Henry?" asked Michael.

"Henry doesn't *do* anything," said Rick. "Except stare."

"He's retaining things in his mind," said Forrest.

"Smile, Henry, smile." Rick grinned a wide, toothy grin.

"Humor him. Humor the kid," suggested Douglas.

"He's *so* little," said Michael.

"His ears aren't. They're huge," Rick said.

"Right," agreed Michael. "Not much hair, but nice ears."

"My finger's getting hot in his hand," said Forrest.

"Hey, isn't this boring," said Douglas. "He doesn't do anything. Ah, Mrs. . . . ah, teacher, we got a baby you can't do anything with."

"Well, I'm going back to Caroline," said Michael.

Frederick had finished his bottle. Seth shifted him over to Smith. Then he got up to stretch his legs and inspect the damp spot on the knee of his pants. "I didn't realize it could be so much fun taking care of babies," he said, "but, oh, my arm. It's done for."

"Boys. Boys. Can I have your attention? The bell's about to ring," said Mrs. Maher. "Next time we'll do diapering, but now please get the babies dressed to go home, and fold up the mats."

As the bell rang, boys from other classes began to mill in the hall outside and peer in through the door. Seth retrieved Caroline's pink jacket and hat from her carriage and gave them to Michael and Rick. "I'll entertain her while you get her dressed," he said. "And hurry! She's starting to cry."

"Boy, this scares me half to death," said Michael.

"I'll do this arm. You do the other," directed Rick. "But be careful. Try not to bend her fingers."

"You have to," said Seth.

"I got a fingey. I got a fingey," said Rick. "Where are the other ones? Oh, there they are. One, two, three, four, five."

"Oh, no," moaned Michael. "She took her other hand out when you weren't looking."

By now the doorway was jammed with boys. "What did you learn? What did you learn?" they wanted to know.

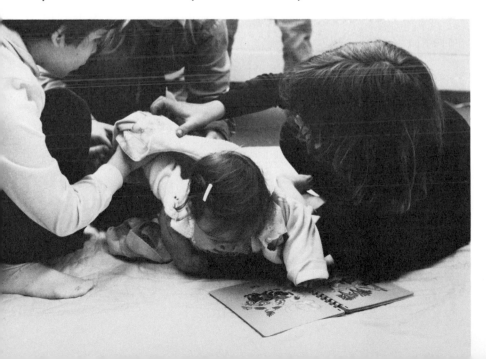

Seth plunked Caroline's hat on her head.

"Well, I can dress them and carry them around already," he answered.

"I wish there was a living soul who would help me with these mats," said Forrest.

The Second Wednesday

Diapering's my favorite. It's hard, especially when you're alone and it's a really rough baby. You need one hand to diaper and one hand to put a toy on top of her head.

— Forrest

The hardest thing? Diapering Andrew.

— Joey

My least favorite part, if I absolutely have to choose one, is diapering. It's kind of icky.

— Dylan

You have to be fast-hands Eddy.

— Gordon

THE BABIES arrived on time for the second class, but the boys were early. They had the desks pushed back and the mats spread before Caroline's carriage came through the door.

"Oh, hooray! It's Caroline!" exclaimed Luke. "Here. Let's push her in."

"I've got her. I want to push," said Rick.

"Boys! Boys! Remember. Keep your voices down," said Mrs. Maher. "Don't charge."

"I'll undress her," Rick said.

"Let me help. She's not *your* baby, you know," said Seth.

Caroline's carriage was mobbed. She began to cry. Mrs. Maher intervened. "Wait a minute. Hold everything. Stop! Don't fight over Caroline. Babies are tougher than you think, but let's not tear her limb from limb. We have lots of babies today. Plenty to go around."

"Is Henry coming?" asked Joey.

"No," said Mrs. Maher. "But Todd's the same age — here, you take him, Forrest — and there's Brooke, a friend for Caroline, and look, here's Freddy. And Andrew. Andrew's only a year old, but watch out, he's a tiger." Andrew was in a backpack. His hair stuck up in spikes.

"A menagerie of babies," said Luke.

"A baby showroom."

"All this year's models."

"Hi, Freddy," said Seth. "Remember me? I'm the one you peed on."

Gordon hoisted Freddy out of his stroller and carried him over to the small mat by the window. "Uh oh, Freddy. You're a big one. You weigh a ton. Twenty-five pounds at least."

Another mother entered the room carrying an oval bundle in her arms. The bundle was Julia in a white, fuzzy bunting. She was the youngest of all the babies, not quite three months old. Julia's mother took Julia out of her bunting and put her in Seth's arms. Michael and Dylan hovered close by, their hands outstretched like a safety net.

"Ah, Miss? Ah. Is it all right for them to be on their stomach?" Seth asked Julia's mother before putting Julia down on the other small mat.

"Can I pull Caroline out of her carriage now?" asked Luke.

"Sure," said Mrs. Maher. "Get a good grip on her, but wait. Undo the safety harness first. I had to buy her one just this morning because she's learned a new trick. She keeps trying to throw herself onto the sidewalk."

"Clever girl," said Luke.

"I broke seven harnesses when I was little," Rick said.

"Shows you how fast babies can change," Mrs. Maher went on. "You have to be quick on the trigger. Stay alert. Find out what your baby can and cannot do."

"I love Caroline's hair. It's sprouting out of her head. It's her image," said Luke.

"There are gubbers coming out of her nose," said Rick.

No sooner had Luke unzipped the harness and freed Caroline than she tried to dive out of her carriage.

"Gotcha," said Luke, catching her under her arms and hauling her up and over the edge. "Did you see that, Rick? She was doing a hurdler."

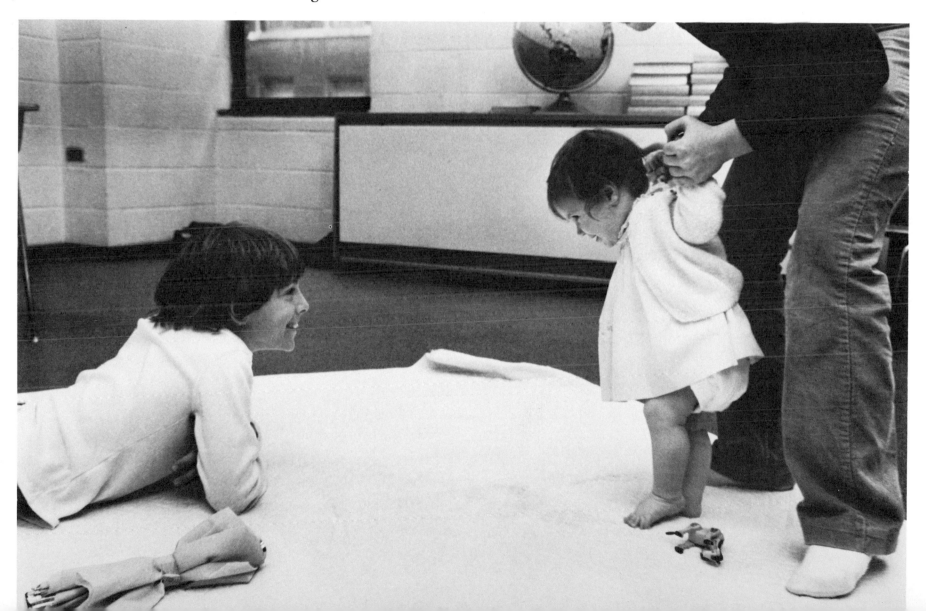

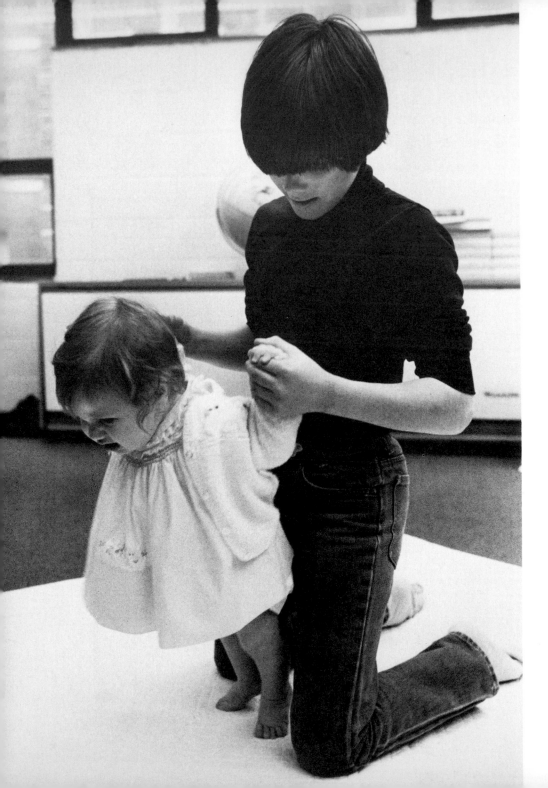

"I wonder if they get muscle cramps the way we do." Rick wheeled Caroline's carriage outside the door. When he returned, Luke had hold of Caroline's hands and was trying to cheer her up.

"Look. She's got tiptoes and she can walk. I taught her. Well, not exactly. It's like she has lead in her feet and just leans forward."

"Good girl, Caroline. Good girl. You're doing great!" encouraged Joey.

"Don't push her along too quickly," advised Rick.

"Did you hear her little tune?" asked Luke. " 'Goggle, goggle, goggle.' "

"Aah, aaaah, aaaaaah," intoned Caroline.

"I like her groaning," said Rick.

Near them Andrew's mother lowered her backpack, and Douglas lifted Andrew out and set him on one of the big mats. Joey went over to help. They took off his sweater and his one-piece yellow suit. As soon as he was stripped to his T-shirt, diapers, and knitted booties, Andrew wobbled like a windup toy toward Julia.

"Oh, boy, this one's a good walker. He needs a leash," laughed Rick.

"He isn't staying on his mat," said Douglas happily. "Don't run away, Andrew. You might get lost."

Rick glanced up at Andrew's mother. "Can I take off her shoes? I mean his shoes. I have this wild urge."

"Look at his legs. He's got muscles all through him," said Gordon.

"Another O. J. Simpson," agreed Joey.

Caroline was still crying. Brooke didn't seem to want to be friends with anyone. She clung to her mother and screamed. Mrs. Maher ignored the noise. "Okay, guys," she said. "What's the most important thing to remember when you're picking up an infant?"

"Support the neck," said Seth. He bent over Julia and felt her hair. "Mine isn't giving me much trouble. You're a very

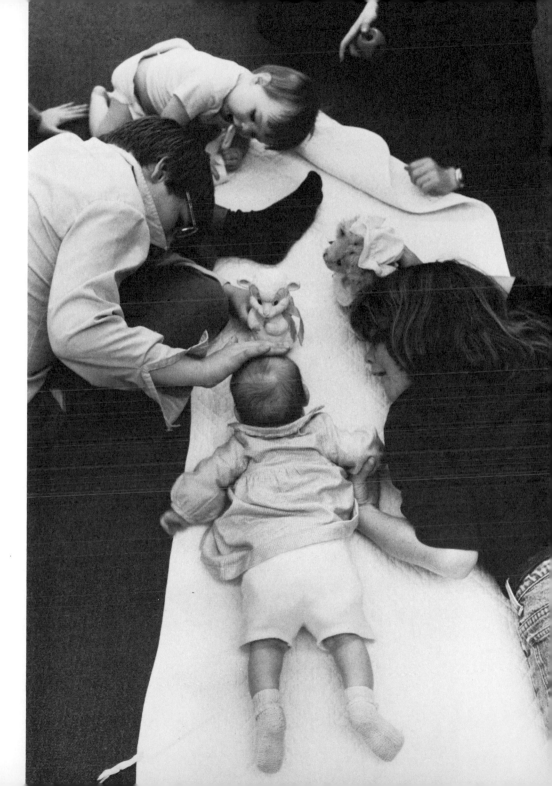

quiet baby," he whispered to her. "You don't make any sounds at all. Just expressions."

"What color are her eyes?" asked Michael.

"Brownish green," said Seth.

"If you put your finger in the middle of her hand, she squeezes it," said Michael. "Want to squeeze fingers, Julia?"

"I never noticed before. Babies have no knuckles. They go in there, like dimples, instead of out," said Seth.

"I was really too young when my sister was born. I didn't know how fun it was, but I remember she held my thumb," said Dylan.

"Boys. Boys. Can I have your attention?" Mrs. Maher had

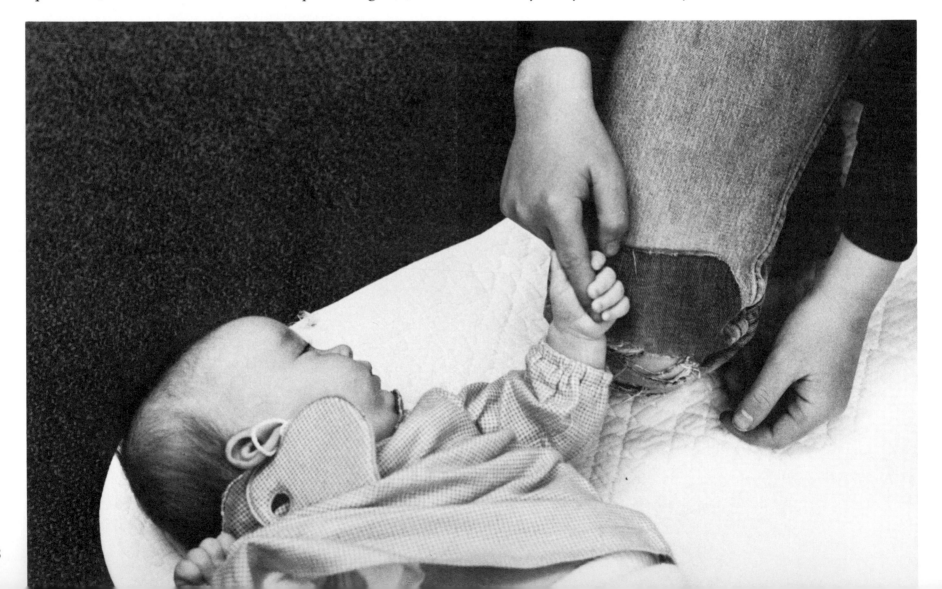

to repeat it. "I know it's hard to hear me because Brooke and Caroline are making so much noise. Some of the older babies are crying because they have grown more aware of their surroundings. They know that they are in a strange place. Give them room to breathe and to move around. Let them get used to your faces. Get to know them. And don't yell. It's like yelling at someone who doesn't speak your language. They can't understand the words, so yelling doesn't help."

Brooke was howling. Caroline crawled determinedly across the mat toward her mother, wailing nonstop.

"Let her go, Gordon. Don't crowd her," said Rick.

"I'm not. I'm just following."

Todd shared Freddy's mat. Forrest gave him a rattle to play with. Freddy yawned and then lay back in Luke's lap.

"Freddy's tired," said Luke. "He just collapsed all of a sudden."

Andrew lurched off on another inspection tour, leaving Joey and Smith to deal with Brooke. Brooke's mother had detached herself and gone to sit on a nearby desk. Joey jangled a ring of plastic keys in front of Brooke's nose, but Brooke didn't even bother to turn her head. She only screamed louder.

"It's hopeless," said Joey. "Do all babies cry this much?"

Brooke gave a horrendous screech and then, without warning, threw herself over backward.

"Oh, disaster!" exclaimed Joey. "She fell. On her head. I missed her." He put a hand over his face and then waved an arm in the direction of Brooke's mother. "I think she bit her tongue."

"I heard of someone in the hospital whose tongue fell out," remarked Forrest.

"She's okay," said Douglas. "You pat her and I'll rub her head."

"How *do* you keep them from falling?" asked Joey.

"Catch them," Douglas said. "The whole thing of it is you have to move quickly all the time."

"Boys. Gather around," said Mrs. Maher calmly. "I'm going to demonstrate diapering now with Caroline. Some people use cloth diapers with pins and rubber pants so the wetness doesn't get through to the baby's clothes. Other people use disposable diapers. You don't need rubber pants or pins with them because they have a protective plastic liner on the outside and tabs for fastening. The tab end of the diaper goes under the waist. Remember, *tabs in back*. But before you put on the new diaper, the baby must be cleaned."

Mrs. Maher foraged in Caroline's diaper bag and pulled out a damp washcloth in a plastic Baggie. Gordon craned over Douglas's shoulder, and Dylan leaned forward. "Boy, are babies fat," he said.

"Look at her little round knee," said Luke.

"Gad, she's hardly got any ankles," said Dylan.

"Okay. Now, Julia gets cleaned off with lotion," said Mrs. Maher. "Andrew's mother uses wipes, and I wash off Caroline's bottom with a wet cloth." Mrs. Maher swabbed her

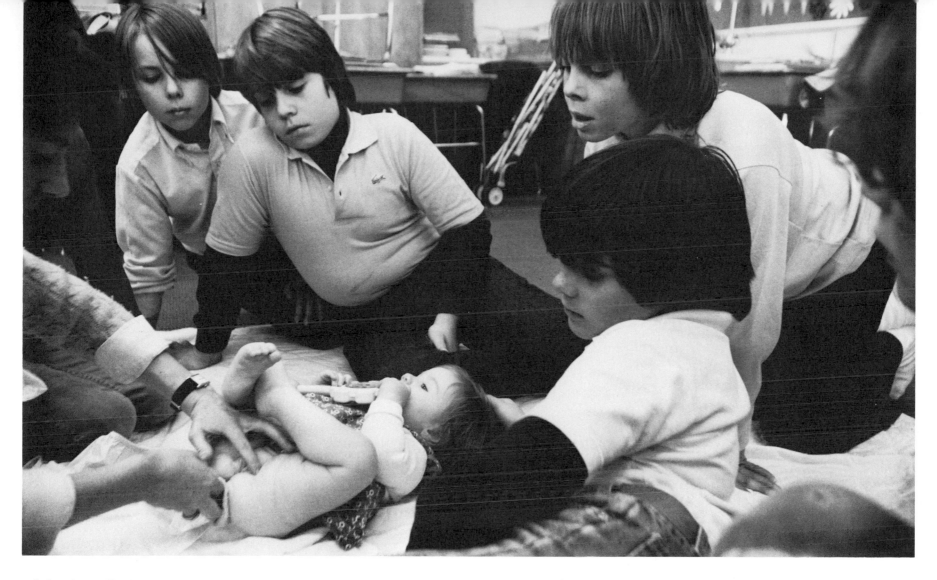

while she talked. "I give her a toy while I'm doing it to keep her entertained, and then I diaper as quickly as possible before she gets annoyed. With little girls make sure you get in all the creases, and whenever you're using pins keep your fingers on the inside between the pin and the baby so if the pin slips it will get you first."

Mrs. Maher removed the disposable diaper she had put on Caroline and went through the whole procedure again using a cloth diaper and pins. Then she doled out diapers to the boys and told them to sort themselves into teams and try diapering different babies.

"I wonder what's in the old diaper," said Joey.

"Do it without touching."

"Maybe use rubber gloves."

"I don't think my mother would want me to watch," said Douglas.

"One more thing," remembered Mrs. Maher. "When the baby stands up, you don't want the diaper to fall down. Put it on tightly. Make sure it's secure."

"Hey, Caroline's mother. Do we have to take the works off?" asked Luke.

"Usually not," said Mrs. Maher. "Nowadays most overalls and playsuits have snaps up the legs so you only have to undo the bottoms."

Freddy was lying down already so Luke and Forrest got his trousers unsnapped and the old diaper off without much trouble. Forrest opened the new diaper and flattened it out. Then he assessed the situation. Freddy was one place and the diaper was another.

"How do you move him along the ground without having to pick him up all the way?" he asked.

"I'll hold up his bottom," said Luke. "Put the new diaper under him. Have you got the tabs the right way? No, you haven't."

"Yes, I have."

"No, they're supposed to be under."

"This tab is stuck, but yours is too tight," said Forrest.

"Oh, I did it wrong. We got to lie him back down again. I got his head. I got his head," said Luke.

"Okay," said Forrest. "Pay attention. Help me. Strap him down."

"You stay here, you little creep."

"Now, Frederick, you're being very difficult with me. I need more diaper. Not too tight. Ah, there she is."

"Oh, jeez. Now all those snaps have to be snapped up again," said Luke.

Seth and Michael rolled Julia onto her back. Michael sang "Silent Night" to her while Seth cautiously cleaned her with little dabs of lotion.

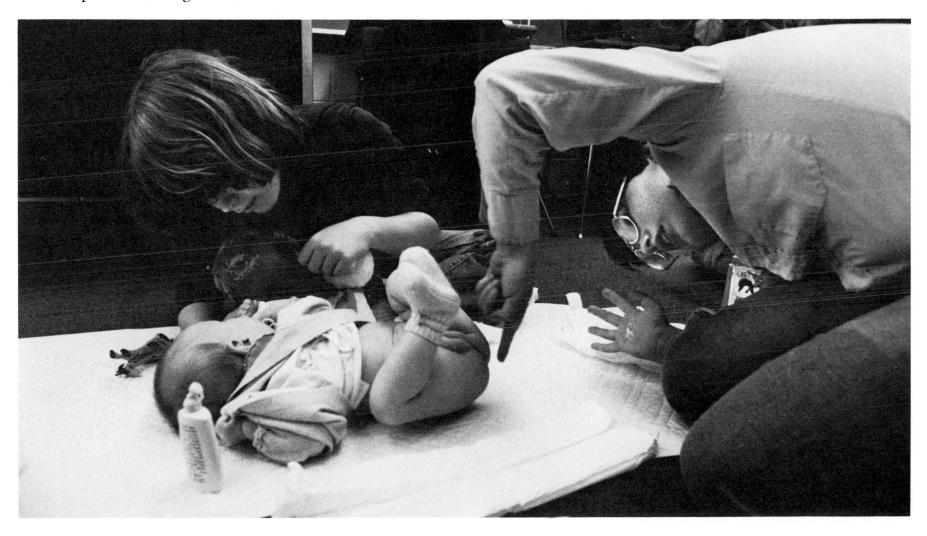

Andrew stumbled across the mats. Joey and Douglas pursued him on their hands and knees.

"Hurry up and catch him," panted Douglas. "We have to get him down. Then I'll entertain him while you change."

"Brooke's got a rash," reported Gordon.

"Sometimes a diaper rash shows a change in body temperature or chemistry," explained Mrs. Maher. "Instead of a fever, a baby gets a rash. Okay? A rash could also indicate an allergy. Brooke's mother discovered that Brooke was allergic to disposable diapers, for example."

"I mean, what gunk do you use?" asked Gordon.

"When I was little I was covered with rashes, and my mother tried Desitin, A and D, Baby Magic, powder, everything," said Rick.

"Keep your legs still, Brooke. Please. I'm not so good at pins," said Gordon.

Caroline did not want to be diapered for a third time, but Smith was determined. Seth crawled over to help.

"I know how to do it now," he said.

"Remember, you've got to get in all the cracks."

"You do it. I don't dare let go of her legs."

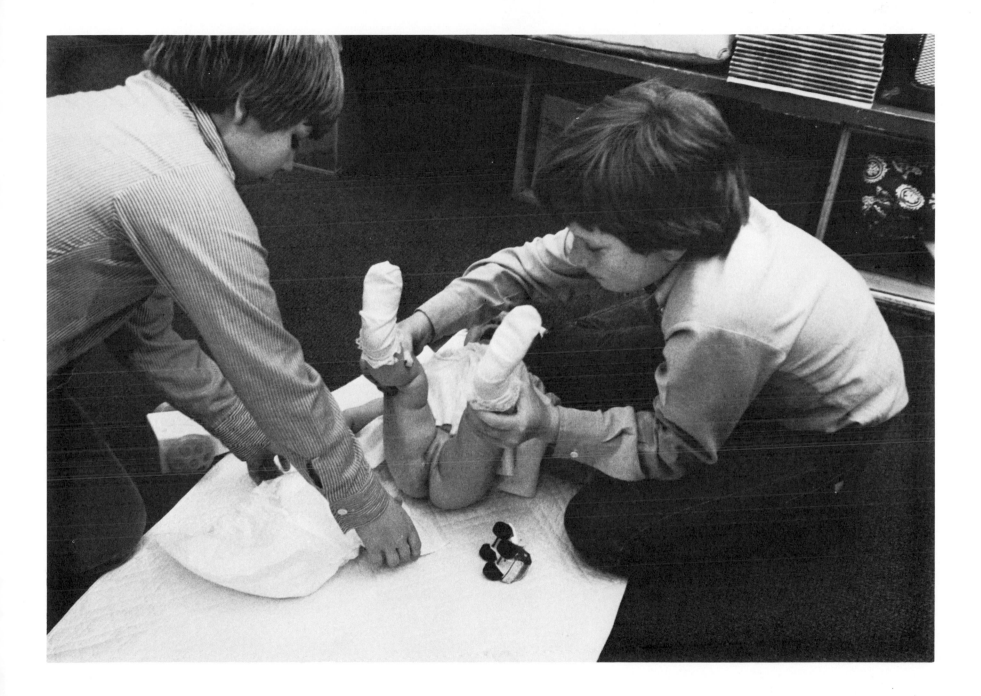

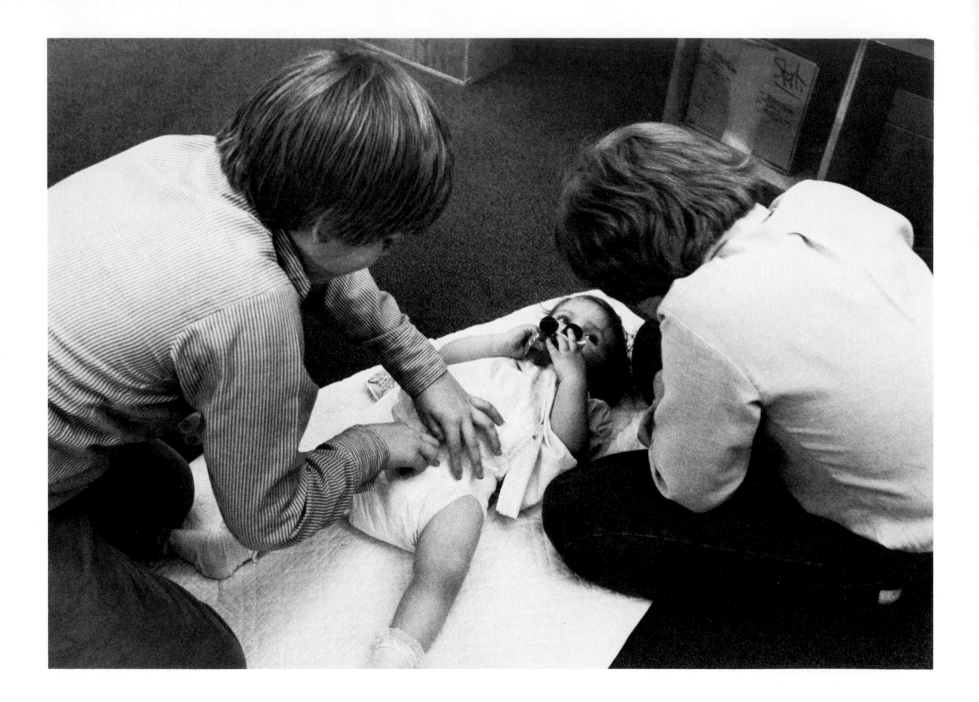

"It's too loose. If this side is too loose, the other side has to be tighter," said Seth.

"Shoot!" exclaimed Smith. "It's falling off after all that work."

Douglas dove for Andrew, but Andrew stiff-armed him and accelerated out of reach. Douglas picked himself up and tried again. "It's no use. I give up," he said.

"Oh, boy," said Joey. "Everything's going wrong. I'll never get the hang of it. Ah . . . Mrs. . . . ah, I think we need a little help over here."

Andrew looked over his shoulder. No one seemed to be after him, so he took time out to observe Forrest changing Todd. Todd's bottom was bare. Forrest scrunched up the old diaper. Todd sucked on his rattle.

"Uh oh! Oh, no!"

"What happened, Forrest?" asked Luke.

"He did a water fountain."

"What did he do?"

"He peed when I took the old diaper off. Maybe because it's cold."

"Did he get you?"

"He got me. On my hand, in my hair. Everywhere."

A boy leaning in the doorway began to laugh. Luke heard him and marched over.

"You're not in this class," he said.

"I'm in 'Wall Murals,'" said the boy.

"Out!" said Luke, closing the door in his face. The boy's face reappeared, pressed against the window in the door.

"You guys. Hey! I think Andrew's done a big poop! Run! Get water! No. Lotion! No. Wipes! Hey, guys, help!" Joey was hanging on to the back of Andrew's T-shirt with one hand; in the other he clutched a tube of Desitin and a toy mirror. A new diaper was clamped under his arm. Luke forgot about the boy peering through the window.

"Hurry up," called Dylan. "Help us get him down."

"Hey, come on, Andrew. Don't kick me, please," said Joey. "He tries to kick and turn over in little parts."

"I can't hold him," said Dylan.

"He's escaping. Don't let him run away," said Luke. "Good, Joey. Now, I stay up here near his head with his toys. You get down by his bottom with the wipes."

Mrs. Maher circled the room checking pins and tabs. She suggested to Smith and Seth that they retighten Caroline's diaper, and she reminded Gordon to put rubber pants on Brooke before he got her ready to go home. Luke and Joey hung on to Andrew, and Dylan entertained him with the toy mirror while Andrew's mother showed them how to diaper a baby who was standing up.

"Diaper changing, baby changing, accomplished," Joey announced to Mrs. Maher. "It's back-breaking work!"

"Wow! That's terrific for a first try," said Mrs. Maher. "Really good. The period's over, but you'll get a chance to practice every week. And next time you're going to learn how to feed."

"I don't need any help dressing Freddy," said Rick. "It's just sneakers and a sweater. It'll be a cinch. I used to have these sneakers. Yeah, tiny." He stuck Freddy's toes into a sneaker and twisted. "Are you sure these are your sneakers, Fred? Hey, Fred, you gotta help me a little." He finally ground Freddy's heel down in and tied the laces. "Next week you're going to get fed. Think you can wait 'til then, Fred? Hum . . . where *is* the front of this sweater?"

When the bell rang, Freddy had both sneakers on, but Rick was still trying to figure out which sleeve went where.

"Bye-bye, Julia. Bye-bye," said Seth.

"Caroline said 'bye,' " announced Luke triumphantly. "Did you hear it? Wave. Everybody wave. Maybe she'll do it again."

"Okay, Andrew. I guess I'll see you next week," said Joey.

"Wait," said Forrest. "Somebody left their rattle and hey, there's a diaper on my desk."

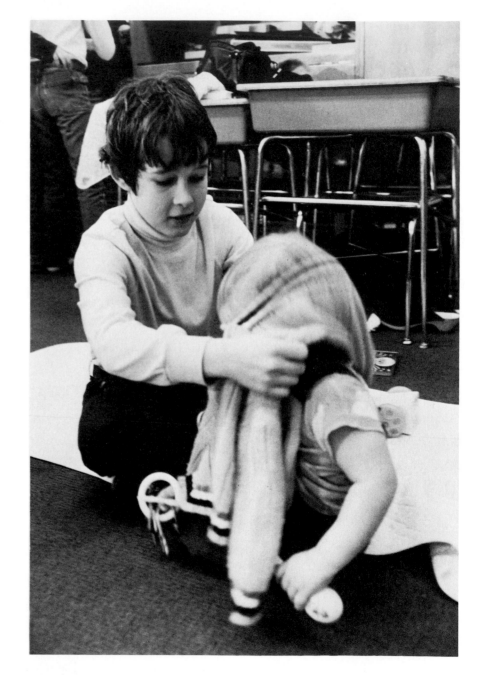

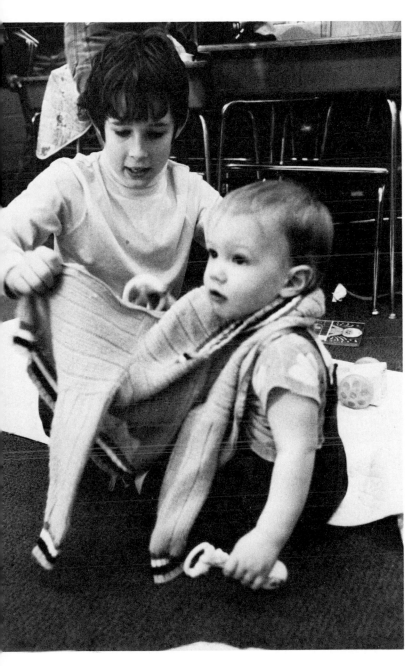
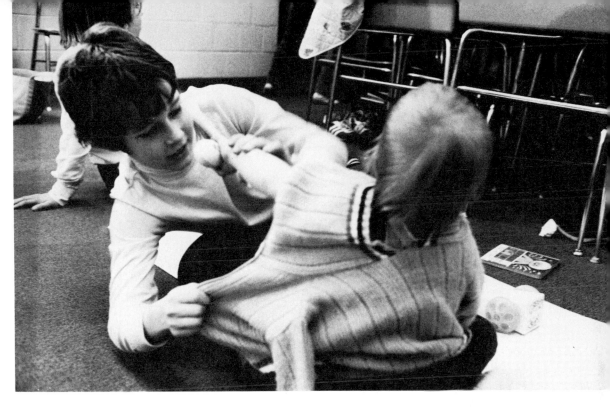
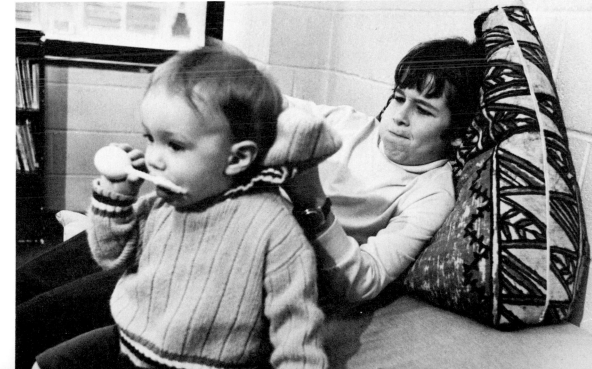

The Third Wednesday

A baby can remember. Take Caroline. When she cries and you give her a bottle, every now and then she'll push the bottle away and go "wah, wah" because she's remembering that before, she was sad and hungry.

— Smith

When I was one year old I remember going to the beach. In July. I remember every single thing about that day. It was nice and warm. I had a hamburger. You might say that my father fed it to me in little bits. And he put Coke in my bottle. And I licked ice cream out of a dish. It was chocolate. I only eat chocolate, even now. I was covered with it. And I made a huge hole in the sand. That's the only thing I remember about being a baby. I pick up again at the age of five.

— Rick

The hardest thing to do? Feed pears.

— Joey

THE THIRD WEDNESDAY Mrs. Maher drove to school with Caroline. Two of the boys met her outside the red door and helped her unload the equipment piled in the back seat of her car. Smith tucked a folding high chair under each arm, Michael took a bag of groceries and Caroline's diaper bag, and Mrs. Maher carried Caroline.

Upstairs in the classroom Andrew was already reeling from mat to mat, and Freddy lay in Rick's lap looking at a book about rabbits. Andrew and Freddy wore matching red-and-white-striped shirts.

"How are you, Andrew? Feeling good?" asked Joey. Andrew sped past.

Seth wheeled Todd back and forth in his stroller. Todd's head drooped until it rested on two double chins and his blinks grew longer.

"I haven't strolled anyone yet," said Forrest.

"You get three more strolls around. Then me," said Luke.

There was another baby near the door. It sat in its mother's lap and smiled and smiled. Some of the boys smiled back.

"Is that a different little baby or the same one?" Joey whispered to Gordon.

"Which is that miniature one? Julia or Henry?" Gordon whispered to Seth.

"I don't think it's either," said Seth.

It turned out to be Emily, a new baby and the youngest one to come to class so far. She was only two-and-a-half months old.

Smith leaned the high chairs against the wall and Michael set the bags on the floor. Mrs. Maher wanted to talk for a minute about babies and food, so the boys put the babies on the mats and arranged themselves around them.

"Douglas will have a fit tomorrow when he finds out he was absent for feeding," said Rick.

"Sssh, you guys," said Luke, patting Todd's back. "Someone's trying to go to sleep over here."

Mrs. Maher kept her voice low. "Very young babies don't eat solid food. When they are born they can either be breast-fed, which is called nursing, or bottle-fed formula."

"Which is better?" asked Seth.

Mrs. Maher considered for a moment, and then she said, "That depends totally on the mother's and father's personalities or situations. Physically, one advantage of breast feeding is that the mother's immunities are passed on to the baby through her milk, but many mothers find nursing confining and some fathers feel excluded."

A boy who had been lurking outside the door sidled into the room and sat down at the edge of the circle as far away from Luke as he could get. It was the boy from "Walls."

"What if the mother gets sick?" asked Joey.

"That's a problem if she's nursing," said Mrs. Maher. "Either the mother has to stop altogether or she uses a breast pump.

Have any of you ever seen one? It's the exact reverse of a tire pump or a gas pump. A breast pump looks like an old-fashioned car horn. It has a rubber bulb on the end of a plastic funnel. When the mother squeezes the bulb, the suction extracts the milk from her breast."

"What do you do with it then?" asked Seth.

"Put it in a bottle. Then the father, or an older brother or sister, can give it to the baby," explained Mrs. Maher. "They can continue to do this until the mother is well again. If the mother stops nursing and doesn't use the breast pump, her body would get the message, 'No one is feeding. I don't need to produce any more milk,' and her milk would dry up. Conversely, the more the baby nurses, the more milk the mother's body produces."

"What if the baby gets sick?" Forrest whispered to Rick. "I once had a temperature of a hundred and four."

"I had a hundred and six," Rick whispered back.

"They gave me Jell-O."

"They always give you Jell-O," said Rick.

Emily's mother leaned into the circle and gathered Emily up. She carried her back to a desk chair by the door, sat down, unbuttoned her blouse, and began to nurse Emily.

"My mother never nursed me. I drank apple juice all my life. It's still my favorite," announced Rick.

Mrs. Maher smiled. "No matter what the baby drinks or whether it is breast-fed or bottle-fed, all babies must be burped until they learn to burp by themselves," she said. "Some of our babies are too young to hold their own bottles, like Henry and Todd. The main trick when you're doing the feeding is to make sure to tilt the bottle just enough so that there is always liquid in the nipple. But no matter how careful you are, they still swallow air along with the liquid when they drink, and air can give them gas pains. Burping gets the air up. Okay? There are three ways to do it."

"Soda water," suggested the boy from "Walls."

Luke leaned back on his hands and peered at him. "Hey, what are you doing here again?" he said in an undertone. "I thought I told you to keep out."

" 'Walls' was canceled. So I decided to do 'Babies' instead."

"You can't. There are too many people here already."

"Can I watch? I've just got to see this."

"No," said Luke. "Well, maybe. If you stay out of the way and don't talk and don't move. And no helping."

Mrs. Maher was demonstrating the three different burping techniques on Caroline. First she held Caroline over her shoulder and patted her back. Then she sat her in her lap and patted her back. And finally she laid Caroline facedown across her knees and patted her back.

"I didn't hear anything," said Dylan.

"Well, she hasn't drunk anything yet," said Mrs. Maher, "and besides, even if she had, she's able to burp by herself. But Emily needs to be burped. You can practice on her. Caroline still drinks from a bottle, but she's also on solid food — meat, vegetables, and fruit that I put through the blender or buy in jars. Her absolute favorite, though, is finger food, like bits of

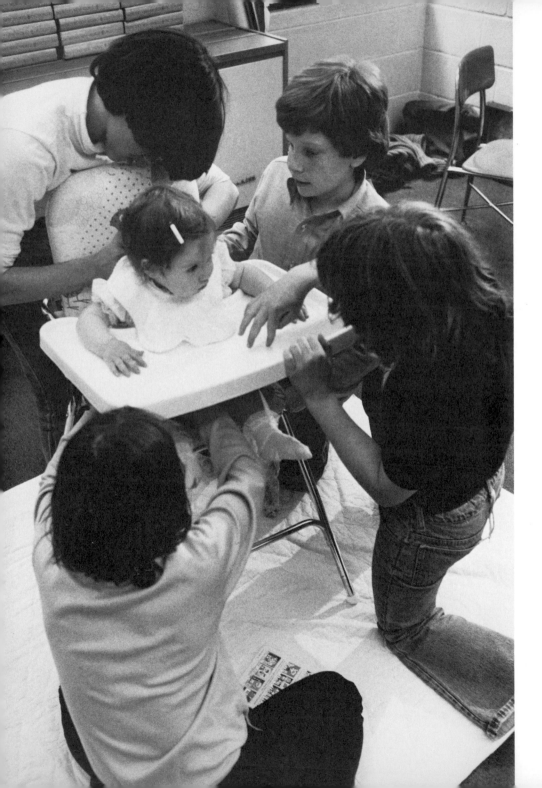

cheese or Cheerios or raisins that she can pick up by herself."

Luke nudged Joey. "She's only got two teeth here and two teeth there," he said.

"There's nothing for it," agreed Joey. "She's got to gum it."

"Do babies like mustard?" asked Forrest. "Because my pants are covered with it. I was aiming at my hot dog at lunch, but I squirted it all over me."

Mrs. Maher was setting out a baby buffet on the teacher's desk: cubes of cheese and wedges of apple, Cheerios and bananas, pears and crackers, several containers of yogurt, small jars and spoons.

"Do you like baby food, Luke?" asked Smith. "Want to try some?"

"Ugh, no. I wouldn't risk my life on it."

The boys set up the two high chairs, side by side. Forrest gently nudged Todd to a safe spot out of the traffic. Todd opened his eyes for a moment and then went back to sleep holding his rattle.

"Take off the tray part. Caroline's coming in," said Luke.

"Watch her fingers," said Dylan.

"Make sure the tray is locked back in place," said Mrs. Maher, "and the safety strap that goes between the baby's legs is buckled before you start to feed. You don't want the baby sliding down and out. And keep the food out of the baby's reach. They love to mush their fingers in it or drop it on the floor."

"Just the smell of this food. Geek! Peaches, vanilla, bananas," said Rick.

"Kind of like a revolting banana split," agreed Joey.

"Get her bag of Cheerios," said Luke.

Michael lifted Andrew into the other high chair.

"No fair!" yelled Rick. "Where are we going to feed Freddy?"

"Sssh. Don't yell," said Seth.

"Feed him in the stroller," said Joey. "Like a mobile diner."

"He'd get carsick," said Rick.

"No, he wouldn't," Seth said. "He never gets anything."

"He's the neatest baby. He smiles and eats and plays and doesn't cry," said Rick. "Here, Fred. Here's a piece of apple. Temptation. Ta da! Then I'll give you some juice."

"Boys, I almost forgot. Andrew's mother doesn't want him to have any sugar, so mash up a banana or a pear," said Mrs. Maher. "And that reminds me — with babies one thing always leads to another — when you baby-sit, questions are important. Ask what the baby eats, how much, in what order — bottle before solids or vice versa — and when the baby should be fed."

Mrs. Maher handed a divided rectangular dish to Smith. Smith filled two compartments with pears and one compartment with banana and then mashed them up with the back of a spoon.

Michael knotted Andrew's bib.

"Andrew's so unhungry," said Gordon. "He keeps turning

his head. Back and forth. Back and forth. It's impossible. I can't get the spoon in."

"Let me," said Smith. "You hold the dish for a while. There. He likes to suck on the spoon. I can feel his teeth grinding on it."

Dylan sprinkled Cheerios on the tray in front of Caroline, and at Mrs. Maher's suggestion, Luke selected a jar of strained pears and a container of vanilla yogurt from the baby buffet. On his way back he stopped to check on Todd. Todd was still sound asleep on the mat by the sink, and Luke stepped over him carefully.

"Okay. I'll try her on these pears," Luke said. He unscrewed the lid and picked up the spoon.

"I don't think she wants it," said Joey. "She's as bad as Andrew. Hey, Caroline. You gotta open your mouth to eat, you know."

"She's got a Cheerio stuck to her thumb," said Seth. "She dropped it in the jar. She's dipping Cheerios."

"Say 'aaah,' Caroline," said Luke, poking at her mouth with the spoon. "Scream."

"Boys, be positive. Be cheerful. Be imaginative. Most parents end up doing the strangest things. Pretending the spoon is an airplane or a motorcycle, singing, standing on their heads." Mrs. Maher danced a few steps and flapped her arms. "Making fools of themselves. Anything to get the babies to eat."

"Oh, scrummmptious!" Smith said to Andrew, running his tongue over his lips and making loud smacking noises.

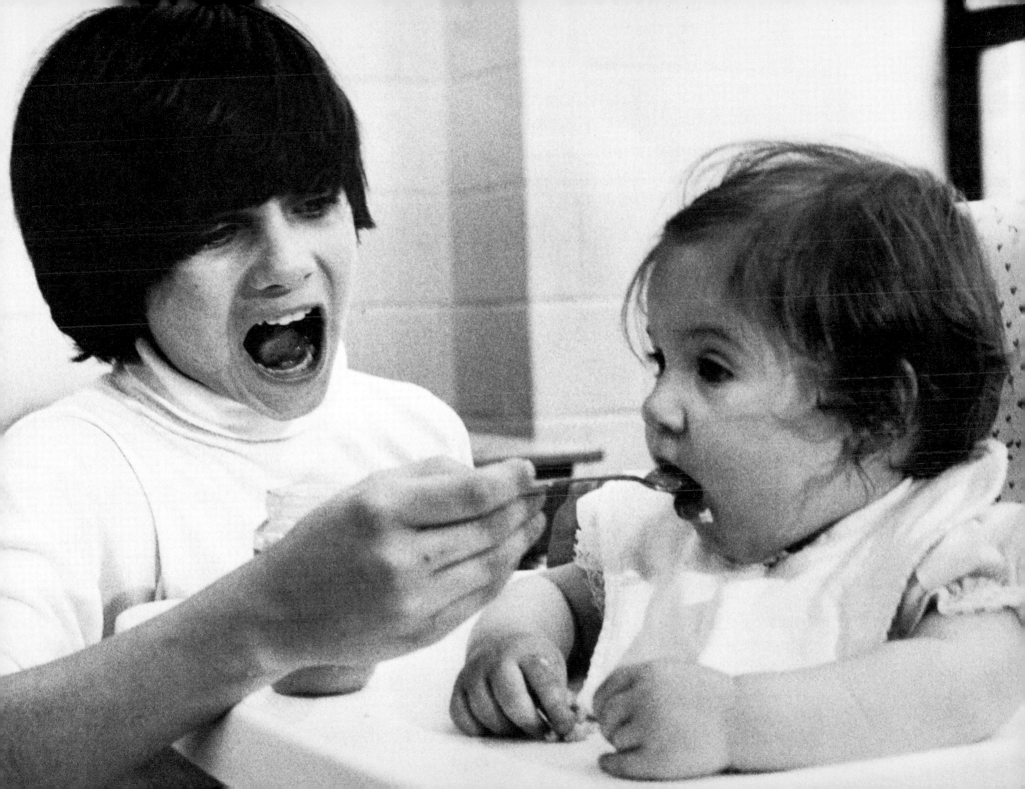

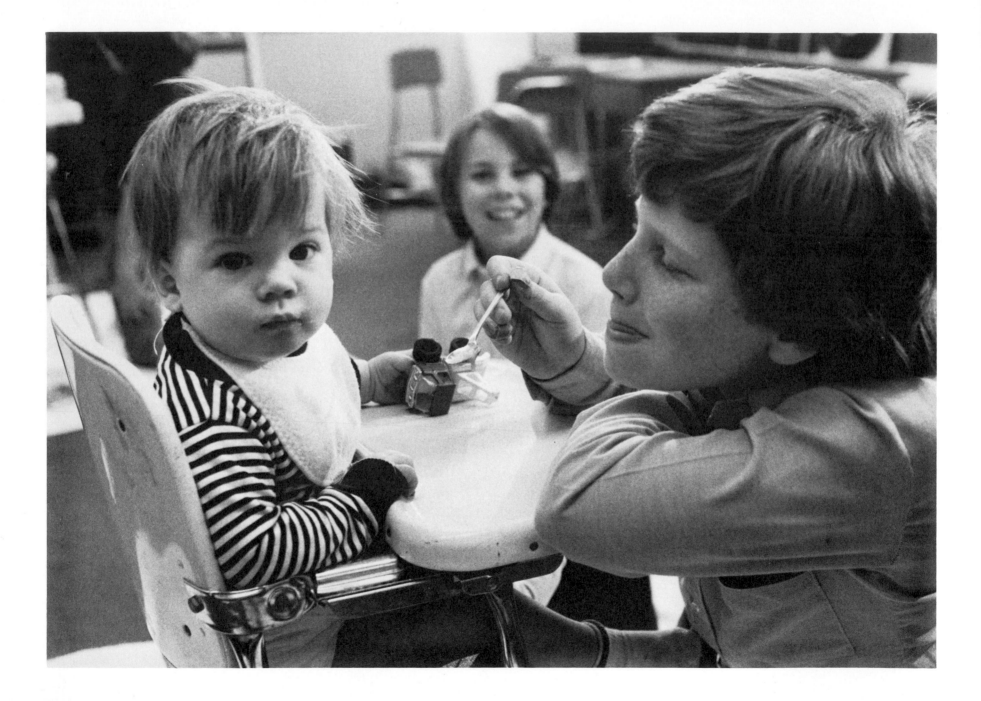

Seth opened the container of yogurt. Luke handed the spoon to Joey, and Joey raised it high over Caroline's head. "Spoony Airlines taking off," he said. "Blip, blip, blip . . . zoom!"

"You're cleared for landing on runway four," droned Seth.

Nee-yaarr-oom. Open up the hangar," said Rick.

"Oh, cripes! She missed," said Joey.

"No. *You* missed," Rick told him.

"Oh, disaster! What if I can't get her to eat? What if she keeps spitting it out?" said Joey. "I'll never make it."

"Scrape it off her chin and shove it back in. You just have to be faster than she is," said Seth.

"You feed 'em, they throw up," said Joey dolefully. "Here, Dylan. Your turn."

"Who took our Cheerio supply?" asked Luke. "What are you doing stealing our Cheerios?"

"I just wanted a few for Freddy," answered Rick.

"Bring 'em back," said Luke.

Dylan offered Caroline a tentative spoonful of yogurt. Unexpectedly Caroline opened her mouth, slurped the yogurt, and then leaned forward for more. Dylan shoveled in yogurt as fast as he could.

"She loves it!" he said in amazement. "Is it okay if she eats the whole thing?"

"Why wouldn't she eat for me?" wondered Joey.

"She's going to live like a Soviet Georgian — 'til she's a hundred and thirty-five," said Luke.

"Oh, gross. I'm covered with baby food. She got yogurt all

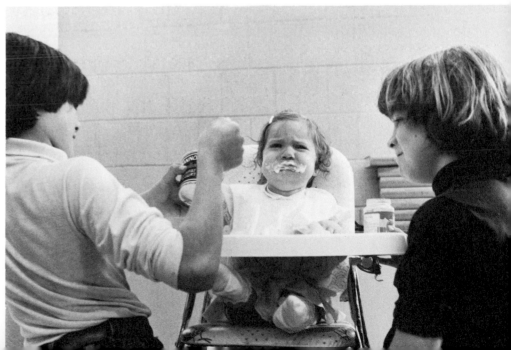

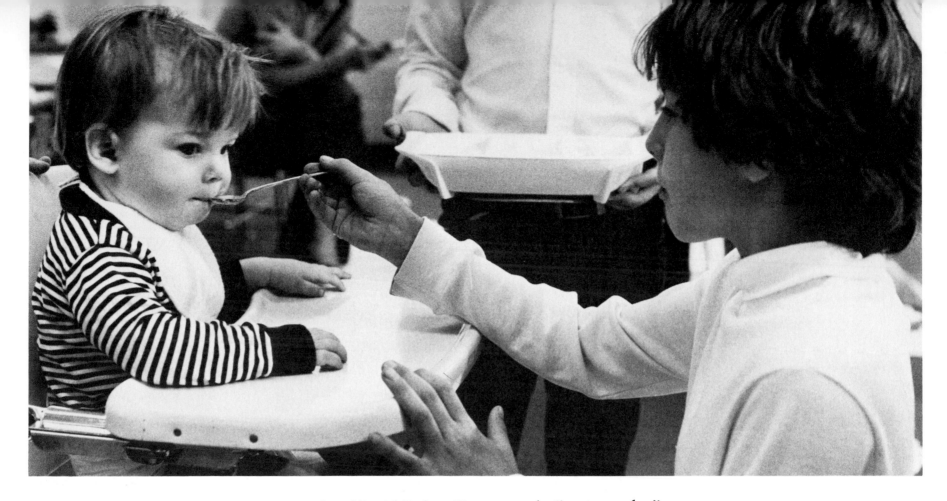

over my hand," said Dylan. "I gotta wash. I'm too yucky."

"You're a messy girl, Caroline," Luke said. "You've stained one of your favorite dresses. No, don't cry. Hurry, hurry, she wants more. Quick! Give me the spoon."

"Don't give her such a wad," said Michael, stopping to watch. He carried an apple in his hand.

"Don't act like such a source," said Luke. "You don't know all that much more about babies than I do."

Joey was trying his luck with Andrew in the next high chair

down. Andrew spat out one mouthful of pears after another and then rolled his lips into a thin line and stretched his neck to get away from the spoon.

"Hey, he said 'nanners,' " reported Smith. "He said 'nanners.' Try him on the bananas instead."

But Andrew didn't want "nanners" either. All he wanted to

do was play with his truck. Finally Smith shrugged and lifted him out of the high chair. Rick heaved Freddy in. Michael locked the tray back in place and began feeding.

Emily had finished half her meal and was ready to be burped. Mrs. Maher beckoned to Gordon and Luke. Emily's mother stood up, Luke sat down, and Emily was deposited in his lap. He tilted her forward over one arm and patted her on the back.

"Did you hear a burp?" he asked after a moment.

"Yes. A little one," said Gordon.

Luke tried again.

"You don't have to pat so hard, Luke," said Mrs. Maher. "Sometimes just rubbing works."

"Want to take over, Gordon?"

Gordon decided to use the shoulder method, so Mrs. Maher draped a diaper over him.

"I got one," he said. "Hey! I got another one!"

"That's a burp? Looks more like throw up to me," said Luke.

"Oh, no! Is it a bad one?"

"It's down your back and in the chair," Luke told him.

"Oh, no," said Gordon again, twisting around to look over his shoulder.

"You got a good burp, and that's only a little spit up," Mrs. Maher assured him. "It's perfectly normal. You don't know how often mothers and fathers have to change their clothes. We'll clean you up in a minute, Gordon. Babies come first."

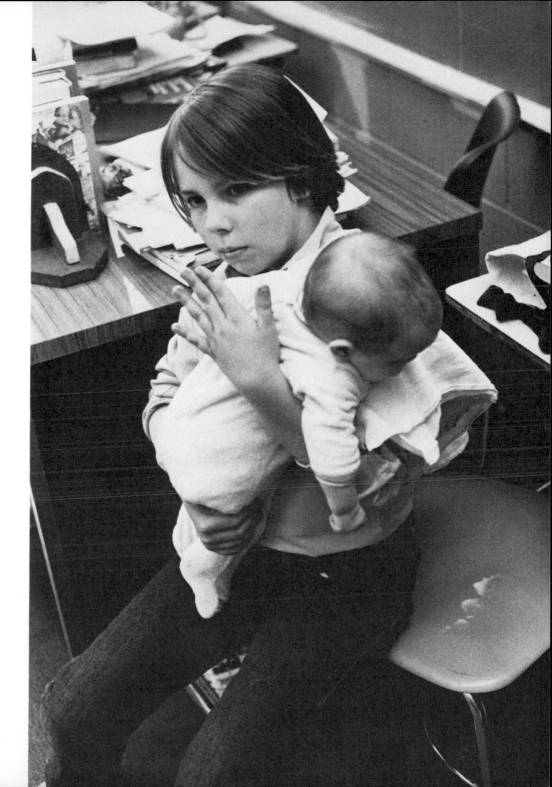

Emily's mother took Emily back and put her to the other breast.

Freddy lounged in the high chair, sucking his bottle.

"Did he eat his apple already?" asked Forrest.

"No. He's sitting on it," said Michael. "I've tried everything. All he wants is the bottle."

"Do we have to burp him?" asked Rick.

"We couldn't even if we had to. He won't let go," Michael told him. "Stubborn little . . ."

"Let him take a breath," said Forrest.

"He doesn't want to. Look at him go!"

"But he's got to breathe," insisted Forrest.

"That's what you think," said Michael. "Try to take it out of his mouth."

"I'll take his shoes off instead," said Rick.

"Okay, boys. We have a lot of loose ends to tie up before the bell," said Mrs. Maher. "Dylan, put Todd's jacket on. Caroline looks like she could use a bath. Michael, why don't you and Seth clean her up. Andrew's diaper is falling off, Joey. It's probably wet. Smith can help you change him. And who wants to put Emily in her front pack? Okay, Gordon. You and Luke."

Since he had to wake Todd anyway, Dylan played a game with him before getting him dressed. "Where's Todd's nose?" he asked. "Where's Todd's nose? Where's Todd's nose? No, silly boy. That's my nose. Where's Todd's nose?" he began again. "Where's Todd's nose?"

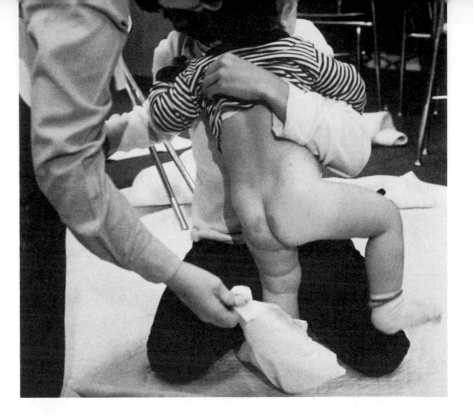

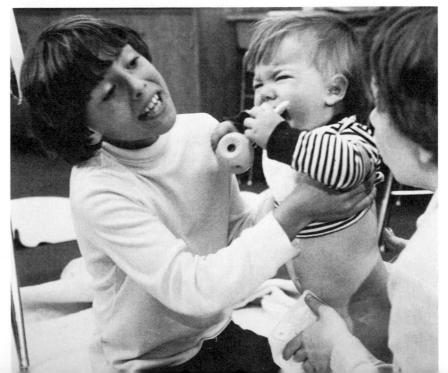

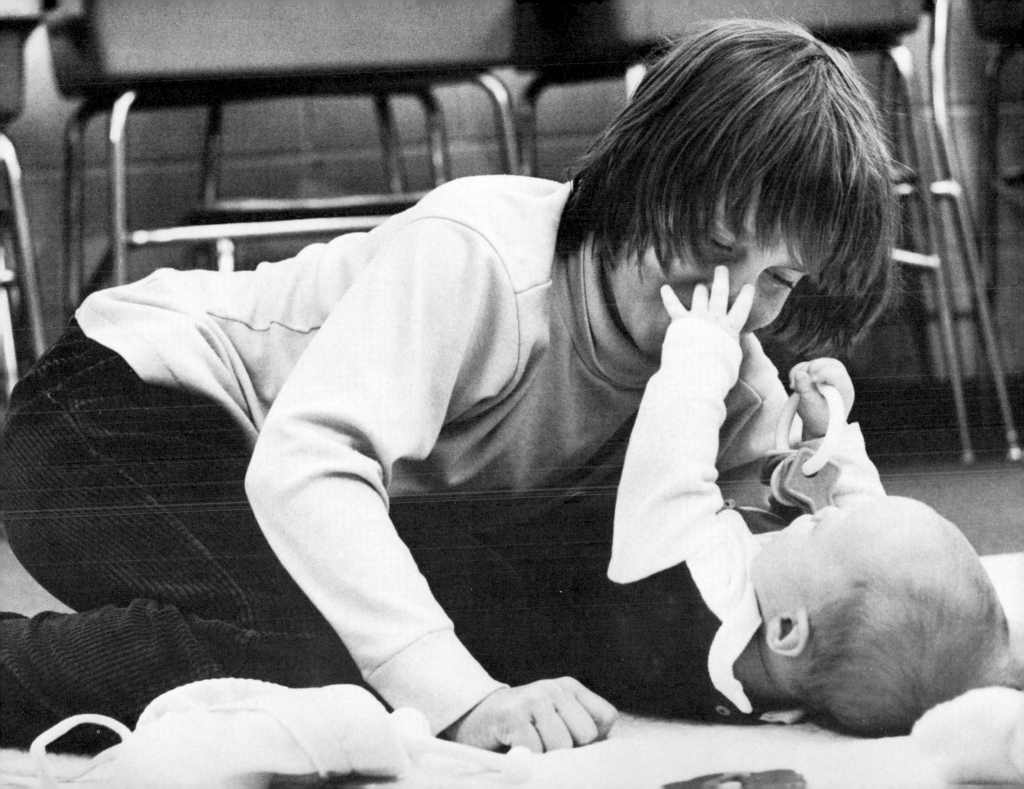

The boy from "Walls" slid off the desk and approached Seth. "I can see why baby-sitters get so much money," he said, watching Joey and Smith struggle with Andrew.

"You don't expend as much energy running four miles as you do taking care of babies," Seth told him. "With babies you never get any time out. You're constantly on the go."

"Look at old Freddy in the high chair. He sure gets into funny positions. He's sleeping with a bottle in his mouth. So even if he wakes up thirsty he won't have to get up," said Rick.

"Excuse me, Mrs. . . . uh. Mrs. . . . uh, Andrew's mother," said Joey. "I think I'm in trouble again. Andrew's bib is knotted and I just cut my nails last night."

For fun, Gordon put on Emily's front pack and Luke fitted Emily in.

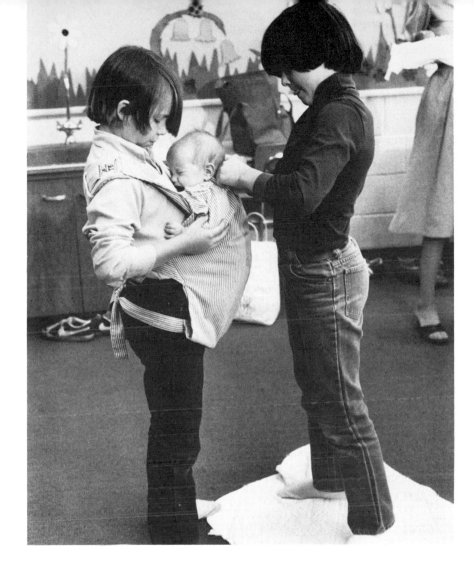

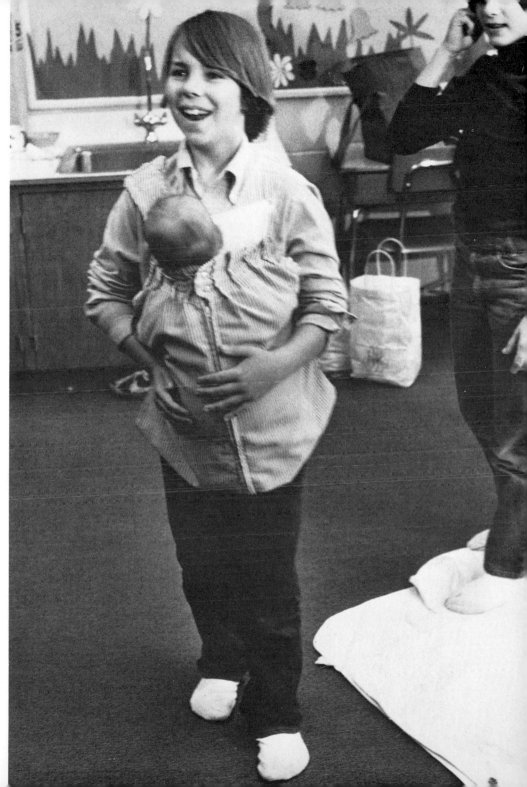

"Does that feel nice? A baby against your tummy?" Luke asked.

"No comment," said Gordon. "I think this thing's too big for me," he added after a moment.

"You look like a kangaroo," said Luke. He stepped back to get a better view. "A Mr. Kangaroo," he said admiringly.

The Fourth Wednesday

What does a baby see when we're looking at the same thing? What does he think? How does he think? I mean, what does a baby think when he sees water, because he doesn't know the word? We see water and we say, "There's water." But what does a baby see? What does he say inside his head? He must invent words for things. But what?

— *Michael*

Taking care of babies is much harder than I thought it would be. All those little details that don't seem important but are.

— *Douglas*

You know, it's much easier to wash a baby than a dog.

— *Luke*

IN THE SECOND-FLOOR BATHROOM at the end of the hall, an empty white plastic tub was balanced on top of one of the four sinks.

"That's too hot! Mrs. uh, Mrs. . . . whatever said babies like lukewarm water," said Michael, testing the water running into the next sink down.

Forrest turned on the cold-water faucet full force. "Perfect," he said. "Now we fill the tubby-wubby."

"How?" asked Smith. "The faucet's too low and the tub's too big. We can't get any water in. And there are no cups."

"And they're showing a movie in the hall," said Forrest. "It's pitch black out there."

Michael ran back to the classroom. "We need a bucket," he said to Mrs. Maher.

"Here's a pitcher instead. And some glasses. You don't need to fill the tub to the brim. The babies aren't that big and they're not that dirty. Four inches deep would be just fine."

When Michael got back to the bathroom, Smith and Forrest had tepid water running in two of the sinks.

"I saw a baby's bath once," said Smith, pouring a glassful of water into the tub. "Not like this one." He dashed in another glassful. Water splotched the mirror. "It was like a tiny box with a chair in it. It was so cute."

Forrest added a second pitcher of water. "For really little babies I think the tubs have these things — headrests — to hold them up." Forrest stepped back and let go with another pitcherful.

"It's a good thing you missed the tub," said Michael. "It's full enough already. Get the other end, Forrest."

The water swelled from one end of the tub to the other and sloshed over the edge.

"Don't get any more on the floor," said Smith. "I've used up all the paper towels."

The bathroom floor was carpeted with them.

"Heads up," yelled Forrest. He inched backward down the darkened hall and into the classroom. "Coming through."

"Slow down! You've already spilled ninety percent on me," said Michael.

"Ooh. My pants are sopped. Stop splatting!"

They set the tub down in the middle of one of the big mats.

"How many babies today?" asked Luke.

"Well, we've got Caroline, Todd, and Henry," said Mrs. Maher. "And I'm hoping for a little surprise."

"Shoot. I hate it when there are tons of people to each baby."

"Don't forget. Rick's absent," said Gordon.

"I know. But we still need more babies."

"You mean Andrew isn't coming?" Joey asked Mrs. Maher.

"No," she said. "I gave him and Freddy the day off. We're short on tubs. We're going to have to bathe Henry and Caroline in the sink as it is. But Andrew and Freddy will be back next week."

"Oh," said Joey. "I was wondering about the certificate."

"This isn't the time to worry about that," said Mrs. Maher.

"But I was just wondering how you keep track of everything. I mean, how we're doing and all. Do you have a book, like a marking book, with all our names in it?"

"I don't need a book," said Mrs. Maher. "I have a pretty good idea of what's going on in the class, and I keep a running score in my head. Now where was I? Oh, yes. . . . Joey, you and Luke and Michael can use the plastic tub for Todd."

Dylan was playing with Todd on the small mat near the window.

"Hi, Todd," he said. "Do you remember I saw you downtown, Todd?" Todd reached up and grabbed for Dylan's hair. Caroline crawled across the small mat, her knees catching the hem of her dress. Henry lay on his back. Every once in a while he caught a glimpse of one of his hands and he stared at his fingers, bending and straightening them slowly, as if they were something he'd never seen before or something that belonged to somebody else.

"Caroline looks ready for a bath," said Smith. "Her dress is covered with crud."

Mrs. Maher handed Douglas some cleanser and a brush and told him to scrub out the sink. While the sink was being cleaned and rinsed, Seth began to undress Henry. Forrest helped. Douglas finished the sink, put in the stopper, and turned on the water. Mrs. Maher stopped him.

"Everyone listen for just a second," she said. "Here's a

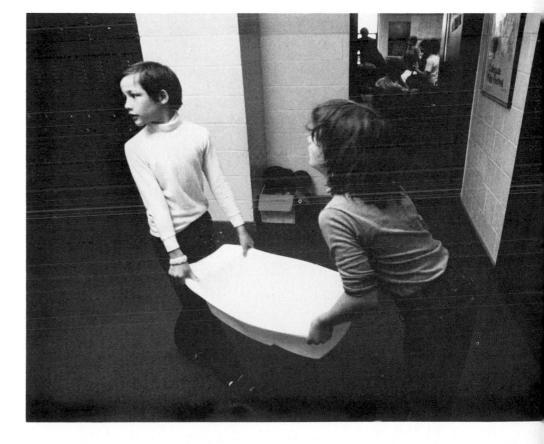

safety trick. Place a folded bath towel on the bottom of what-ever you're using as a tub so the baby won't slip. Now, I'm going to show you how to hold a baby while you give one a bath. I'm going to use Henry, although ordinarily he prefers to lie flat in shallow water."

Douglas turned on the water again and tested the tempera-ture.

"Do we have to take his diapers off?" asked Forrest.

"Everything," said Mrs. Maher.

When Henry was stark naked, Forrest handed him over. Mrs. Maher lowered Henry into the water. Henry looked startled. He gave a little shiver.

"Okay," said Mrs. Maher. "I hope everyone can see. I lean the baby back against my left arm to support his neck. My left hand goes around the baby and grasps his upper arm. See?"

Dylan climbed up on the counter to get a better look.

"Keep a firm grip on his arm. Wet, soapy babies are very slippery, like greased piglets. Now. My right hand is free to work. Start with the face and wash the eyes first. Use only wa-ter, and clean them from the inside corner out. Got that? Then you soap up the cloth and wash the rest of the baby just like you would yourself. Some mothers use Q-tips either before or after the bath to do their ears and noses, but if you use them, be very, very careful not to stick them in too far. Okay? Dylan, Seth, take over here. The rest of you move back."

"I've gotta roll my sleeves up," said Seth.

"Does that feel good, Henry? In a hot room like this?" asked Dylan. "I'd love to have a bath too."

"Did you get the inside of his eyes?" asked Seth.

"Yup. Behind his big ears too."

"Look," said Seth. "He loves having water dribbled on his head and tummy."

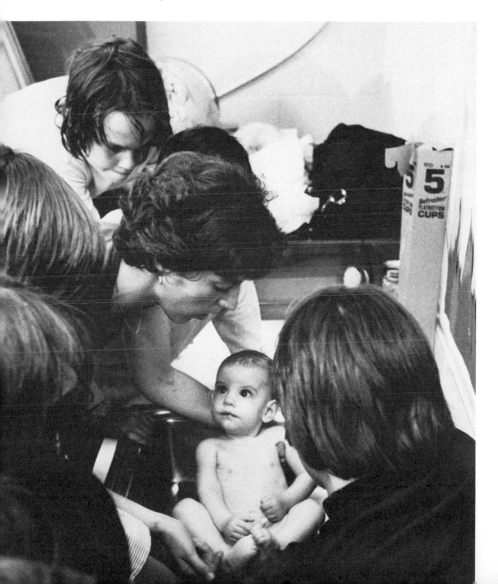

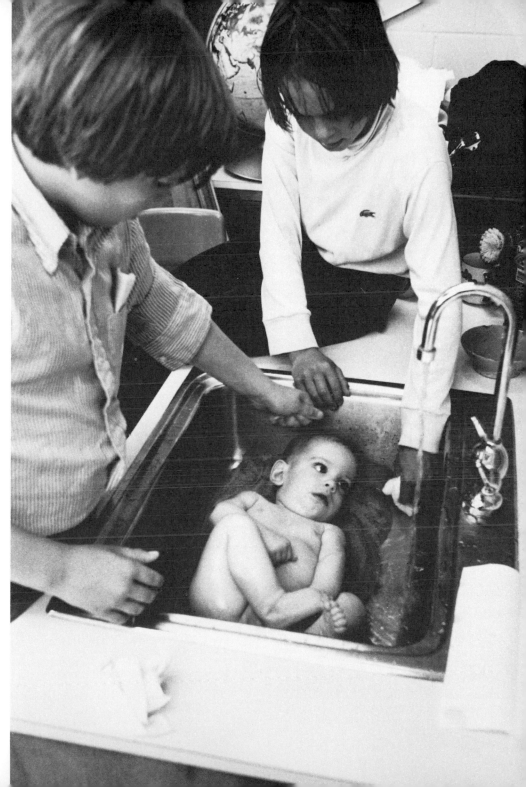

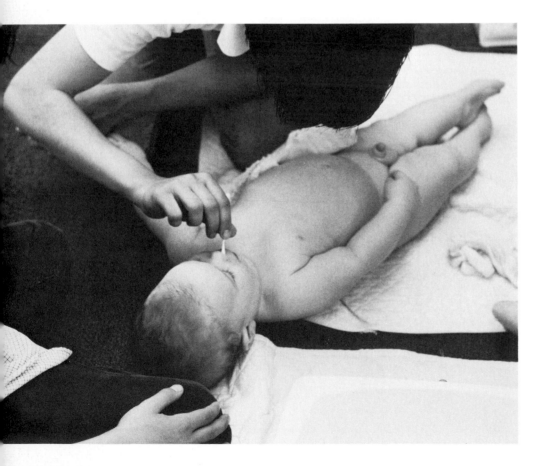

The mat around the plastic tub was cold and damp. Joey checked the water in the tub to see if it was still warm enough. But before Todd went into his bath Luke carefully cleaned his ears and nose with a Q-tip.

"He feels really unsure," said Joey. "That's why he's crossing his legs."

As soon as Todd was in the water he began to kick.

"Good grief, he's doing calisthenics. Or laps," said Michael.

"I think he could swim to New Orleans," said Joey.

"You're slipping, you're wiggling, you're impossible," said Michael.

"Keep his head up," said Luke.

"I am. I am," said Michael. "Oh! Dis*gust*ing. . . . Water all over me."

"You're doing just fine," said Mrs. Maher, checking in on them, "and Todd's got it made. Most babies think baths are playtime."

"But remember. The number-one thing," said Luke. "Do not drown the baby."

"What if he flips over?" asked Joey. "On his face? In the water?"

"He can't," answered Mrs. Maher, "because you never, never let go. And you keep an eye on him all the time. Cleanliness is second to safety."

Only Forrest noticed the arrival of the little surprise. It was a baby boy, so small that he was barely a lump in his front pack, and his head, sticking out the top, was no bigger than an ostrich egg.

"Who's that?" asked Forrest.

"His name is Rami," said Mrs. Maher, "and we're very lucky. He's only six weeks old. I'd begun to think he wasn't coming. He's here for a visit, not a bath."

"Hey, Doug, we got a six-week-old baby," said Forrest.

Rami's mother hesitated. She looked around for a moment. Dylan and Seth were giving Henry a shampoo in the sink; in the middle of the room Michael supported Todd's head well out of the water in the plastic tub while Joey and Luke took turns lathering and rinsing. Rami's mother unzipped the front pack and gave Rami to Douglas. Douglas carried him confidently, one hand under his bottom and one hand supporting his head, to the mat near the sink. "He's lighter than the other babies," he said. Mrs. Maher came over to admire him.

"The top of his head's going up and down," said Douglas. "As if it's breathing."

"What you're looking at is the pulse in the fontanel," explained Mrs. Maher.

"The what?" asked Forrest.

"The fontanel. The hole at the top."

"Hole?" asked Forrest.

"Yes."

"Really a hole?"

"Yes," repeated Mrs. Maher. "It's an opening between the bones of the skull covered only by membrane."

"Oh, gross, sick. It's repulsive," said Douglas.

"It's neat," said Forrest.

"I don't have one, do I?" asked Douglas.

"Not anymore. Yours has closed. The bones have grown together," answered Mrs. Maher.

"When does that happen?" asked Forrest.

"It's different in each baby, but usually before it's a year old," said Mrs. Maher. "Until that happens you have to be very careful of that place."

"Why would a baby have a hole in its head?" asked Douglas.

"So the head can contract when it's being squeezed through the birth passage. Before the fontanel closes you can see as well as feel the baby's pulse there."

"He's really cute," said Forrest.

"He's got zits," said Douglas. "He's been eating too much chocolate."

"Oh, cool! We get to diaper him. And everything," said Forrest.

Henry had been washed from head to toe twice. He was ready to come out of the sink.

"Wet babies get cold quickly," cautioned Mrs. Maher. "So when you take them out of the bath, have a towel ready."

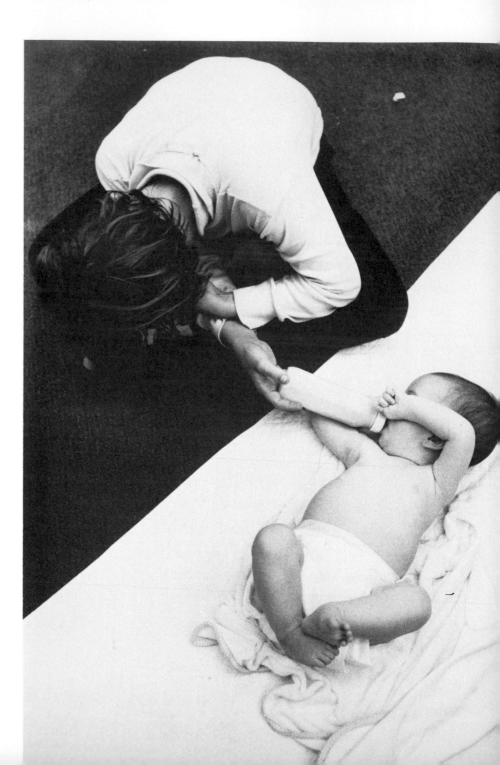

Seth dried Henry off and Dylan put him in a clean diaper and fed him a bottle.

Caroline had on a lot of clothes that had to come off: sweater, dress, tights, undershirt, and diapers. Gordon ran fresh water in the sink and respread the safety towel. Caroline did not want to lie down in the water. She didn't want to sit down. She didn't want to be in the water at all. All she wanted was to climb out onto the counter. Smith produced his collection of baseball cards to entertain her.

"Gotta get under her chinner," he said, waggling a card in the air. "Here, Caroline, here. Quick, quick! Get her while she's looking up. Uh oh! My baseball card. It fell in."

"I'll do this side," said Gordon. "You do that side."

"She's got fuzzies between her fingers," said Smith.

Caroline tried to pull her hand away. She looked cross and miserable.

"Hey, Caroline. Don't cry. You don't want to be clean?" said Gordon. "Well, look at it this way. It's the first step to a manicure."

"Her hands are getting all wrinkly. I think she's done," said Smith.

"I'll get the towel ready."

"Hurry, hurry. She's sneezing. Get the sneezy cloths," said Smith.

"Uh oh, crying. Ssh. Ssh. I know it's a terrible world," said Gordon.

"Get her bottle," ordered Smith.

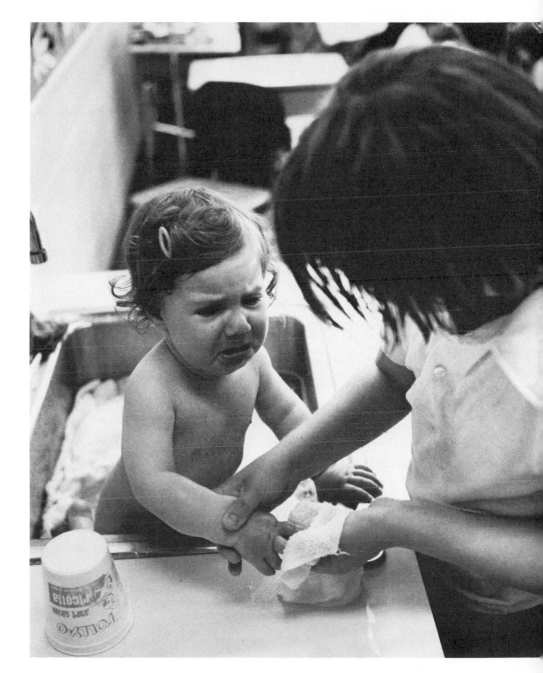

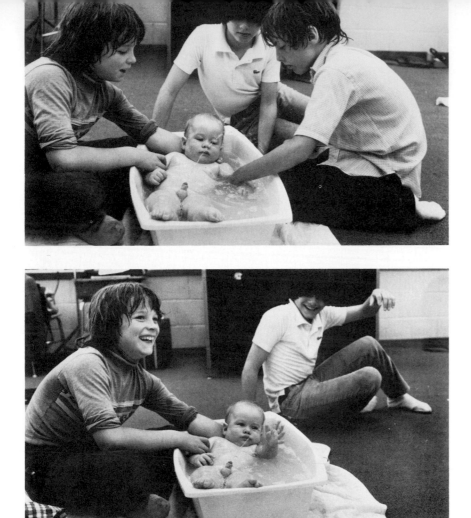

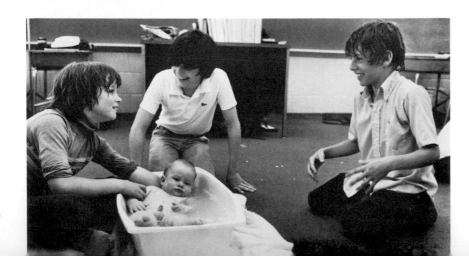

"That's what we wanted, didn't we? The bottle does it every time," said Gordon. "Got to make sure there's a lot of milk in the nipple."

On the other side of the room, Joey had washed his way down to Todd's feet. "I'm finished with that toe," he announced.

"Hey, Joey? Has your mother had your baby yet?" Michael asked him.

"No. And she fell down in the yard. But the baby wasn't hurt because it's surrounded by water. So it's still in there sloshing around."

"What's the temperature in there?" asked Luke.

"Uh . . . uh . . . warmish," said Joey.

Just at that moment Todd peed a high arc. Joey flung himself out of the line of fire.

"Did he get you? Did he get you?" yelled Luke.

"Another water fountain," said Michael.

"Wasn't Todd the one who did it last time?" asked Luke. The three boys beamed at each other.

"Hey, Todd," said Joey. "That was some super job."

Rami shared a mat with Caroline. His legs were thin and bent.

"Look," said Mrs. Maher. "You see. His legs are still scrunched up from being inside his mother."

"Can he cry?" asked Smith.

"He sure can," answered Douglas. "I thought it was going

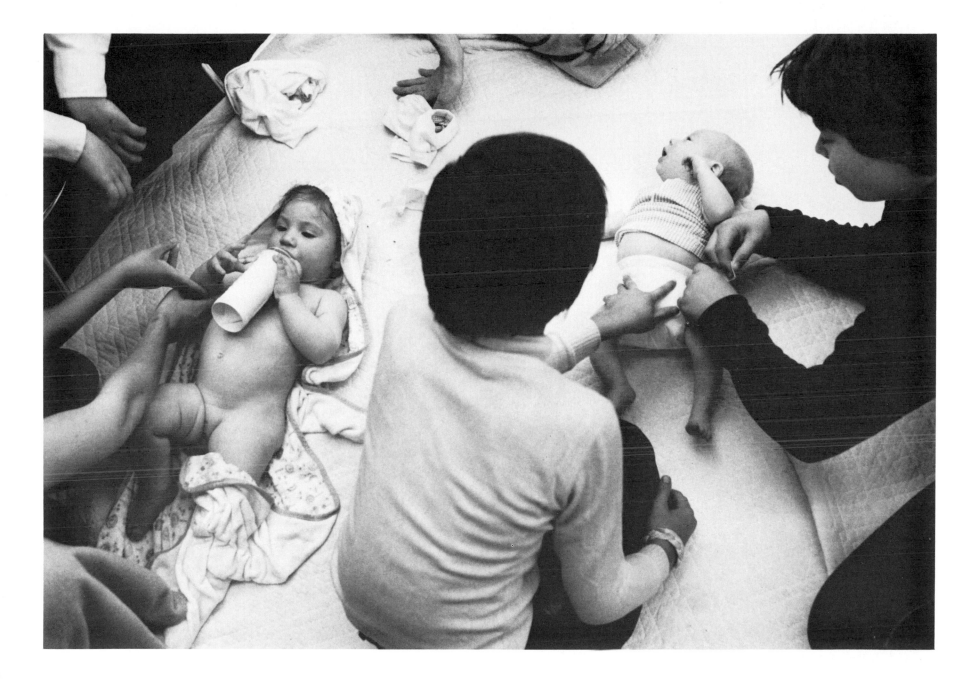

to be harder to diaper him with his legs like that. But it's easy. He unbent them."

"My parents taught me to walk too early," Forrest said. "So I got pigeon-toed and knock-kneed. But I'm all straightened out now."

"His toes are so weeny," said Smith. "They look like they're stuck on."

Gordon finished diapering Caroline. "I don't think her legs were ever as little as Rami's," he said.

"Look at her thighs," said Seth. "Pudgy. Pudgy. Pudgy. Flab grab."

"Oh, gosh. Now, we've got to dress her," said Smith. "What are these stocking things?" He held them up and turned them over.

"They're not stockings. They're tights," said Seth.

"They're worse than stockings," said Smith.

"She just wet again," said Seth.

"Forget it," Smith told him.

"Okay. Here goes."

"Oh, jeez! This is going to be impossible," said Smith. "Get down in there, foot. I have one whole leg on."

"Boy, are these tights tight."

"Let's see. . . . The dress . . . goes, uh, . . . over her?"

"Obviously," said Seth. "You can't stuff her feet down the neck. Oh, watch it. You're wiping her face off with her dress. And do the buttons go . . . in back? Are you sure?"

"Is it on backward?" asked Smith. "Oh no! We put the dress on backward."

"You idiot! *You* put the dress on backward."

The babies were almost ready to go home. Todd was dried and in his checked playsuit. Luke and Michael emptied the soapy water from the plastic tub into the sink, while Joey struggled with Todd's socks. "Come in, foot. You need your sock on. Come in. Done. I wish somebody would put my socks on like that," he said.

Forrest and Douglas zipped Rami back into his front pack. Dylan dressed Henry and finished giving him his bottle. "Henry's so sweet. I love those big brown eyes staring at me," he said.

"What happens next week?" Seth asked Mrs. Maher.

"Fun and games," she told him.

Seth and Smith swiveled Caroline's dress right way around.

"If she tilts her head forward, I can't button," said Smith. "I still can't button. C'mon, button. C'mon. I don't believe it. They keep undoing."

"You could take a movie of this whole thing," said Gordon, "and no one would believe it."

The Fifth Wednesday

A baby doesn't have to work around the house. All those toys that he has; he can play with them without being called a baby.

— *Forrest*

Being a baby is tough. You get changed when you don't want to be, fed when you don't want to be, given toys you can't do, put to bed when you're not sleepy. You can't run your own life. Everything is done for you. Of course nothing is done for me. And I have so much homework I can't go out and play. I can't run my life either. Each of us has our hardships.

— *Smith*

Being a baby is better than school. Just to sit back and let everyone else do things for you is nice. Sometimes when I'm passing a playground I used to be in, I go there and climb around the swings.

— *Dylan*

A baby's life is great. It gives you experience at being young.

— *Douglas*

BOYS! BOYS!" Mrs. Maher stopped doling out toys from a huge canvas carryall and straightened up. She held both hands in the air as if she were directing traffic. "Boys, come on! Can I have your attention, please. We've got to get down to work now."

Rick blew another string of bubbles over Todd's head.

Luke didn't look up. He sat on the floor next to the carryall playing with a painted wooden bus.

"Oh, I remember this," he said. "I had one once. With the little people that fit in the holes. I used to play with it in the bathtub."

"I hated those toys," said Rick.

"Oh, I loved them."

Douglas and Forrest wanged each other with a stuffed hammer and a calico screwdriver. Joey peeked through the windows of a plastic keg and Seth examined a jack-in-the-box.

"I could never figure this out, but now, I see," he said to himself. "There's this big latch inside that lets go."

Dylan commandeered a fat-wheeled plastic kiddie cart and began to trundle himself around the room. The dashboard of the cart was a bright red apple with black bug eyes as headlights.

"I'm next," said Forrest.

"No, I called it," said Smith.

"Hey, boys. Listen. Toys are fun, I know, but they're not just for fun. They're to entertain and to educate." Mrs. Maher paused for emphasis. "The babies, *not* you," she said. Joey peeked through the windows of the plastic keg at Todd. "Play is a baby's work. Babies are really learning when they play. So it's important that you give babies toys appropriate for their ages. Ones that will challenge without discouraging them. For instance, do you think a rattle would be a good toy for Andrew?"

Nobody answered. Andrew watched his cart roll by and began to cry. Dylan drove up to each baby in turn and beeped the horn twice. "Hi, Caroline. Hi, Freddy. I mean, Todd. Sorry. There are so many babies today."

"Don't forget Brooke," said Forrest. "Give her a beep, too. Then it's my turn."

Brooke buried her face in handfuls of her mother's skirt and wailed. Caroline gave up crawling toward her mother. She planted herself on all fours, hung her head, and howled at the mat.

"Everyone's crying today. What's wrong?" asked Joey.

"Oh, Caroline, I love you. I just love you. But I wish you'd cut the noise," said Luke.

"It's not a noise. It's a screeeeeam," said Forrest.

"Don't let her see her mother," Smith said.

Forrest lay on his back in front of Caroline and looked up

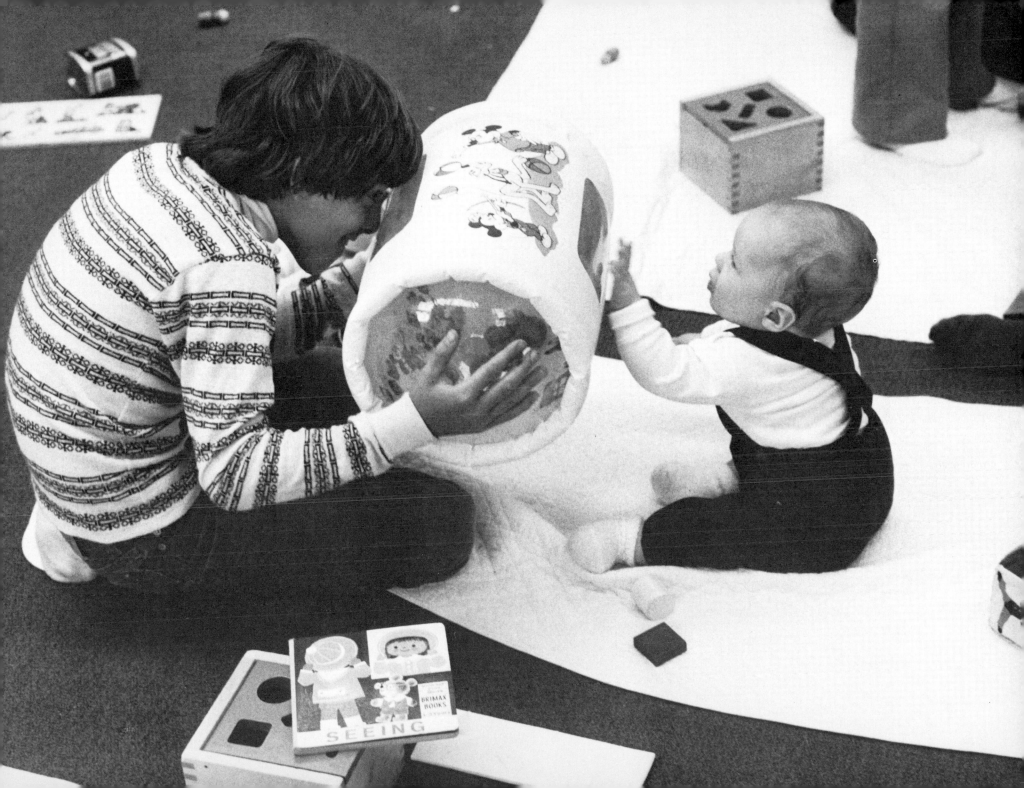

into her face. "I know. Next time I'll bring in a wig and pretend to be your mother."

"The solution to all our problems," said Luke, "is to get rid of the mothers."

"Boys, you're smarter than these babies. Outwit them. Distract them. Get their attention off their miseries and onto their toys," said Mrs. Maher. "Play with *them*. Not with each other."

"Yeah, Dylan. Give Brooke a ride on the big apple thing," said Seth.

"This thing is neat. I wish I'd had one when I was a kid." Dylan propelled the cart back to Brooke and got off reluctantly.

"First let her see it," advised Mrs. Maher. "Let her get used to it. Just suggest it. Then she'll decide whether she wants to ride or not. Try to find toys that will stimulate the babies. Sort of build their self-esteem."

"Want a rattle, Freddy?" asked Douglas.

"I wouldn't give him a rattle," said Seth. "It wouldn't occupy him at all. Try it on Todd. He likes to chew things."

"Got to give something to Freddy. He's just sort of hanging out," said Michael. "I know, a ball. A ball is good."

Mrs. Maher was holding up her hands for attention again. "There are good toys and bad toys. What do you think would be a bad toy for a baby?"

"Pop guns."

"Something electric."

"Something dirty."

"Laundry," said Forrest.

"Something sharp."

"Carving knives."

"Chessmen."

"Monopoly. They'll eat the hotels."

"Small things they could swallow."

"Things that come apart in little pieces."

"Teddy bears. I ate the eyes off mine."

"Dinky things that splinter easily."

Mrs. Maher held up a blue football. "Is this a good toy?"

"Great!" said Michael. "Toss it here."

"I don't know," said Joey. "They could eat it."

"You're crazy. It's too big."

"No, I'm not. Look. There are bites out of this one. Everywhere."

"Joey's right," said Mrs. Maher, "because that football is made out of Styrofoam instead of leather. Never buy Styrofoam toys. Babies love to chomp on it. For that matter, many toys don't need to be bought at all. You just find them around the house. What might you find for a baby to play with in the kitchen, for example?"

"Pots and pans?"

"And ice cubes. In the summer. That's nice," said Rick.

"Wonder if babies like snow," said Forrest.

"Maybe a spoon? No. They'd swallow it. Maybe a *big* spoon," said Joey.

"And napkin rings, pot holders, measuring spoons, plastic containers that fit inside each other, to name a few more," said Mrs.

Maher. "But don't inundate them with too many toys at once. Let them play with one or two at a time. Rotate the toys. Put some away and bring out others. They'll think the ones they haven't seen for a while are new. Or you can exchange toys between babies. Here. Let Andrew try Freddy's puzzle box."

"Have you got a ball I could give Freddy?" asked Michael. "He likes balls. He throws his apple wedges."

Mrs. Maher delved into her bag of toys.

"Oh, we get new toys, Caroline! Isn't that exciting?" said Forrest. He slid the jack-in-the-box under Caroline's nose and began to wind the handle.

"Not so close, you idiot. It'll pop up and kill her," said Luke.

The turning of the handle plinked out a tinny tune. Caroline stopped crying and eyed the box suspiciously.

"Okay. Okay. Wait," said Forrest. "I know it's fun. But you've got to wait until I stop turning. She's getting ready to attack it. She likes wrecking things. Wait! Wait! It doesn't pop up yet. Bingo! There it goes! Hey, she loves it!"

"Um be de gum, be de gum, be de gum," said Caroline.

"She says that every time she sees me," said Forrest. "I think she knows me. She's beginning to look just like my sister."

"We ought to get some of these toys. I could sit around playing with them all day," said Luke.

"I love these toys. They're more fun than our toys," said Forrest. "I love these pop-up boxes. I still have mine."

Near the teacher's desk Rick propped Todd in a sitting position and showed him how to work a busy box. Rick

twirled the dial, pulled out the drawer, squeaked the horn, slid the car back and forth, and made faces in the mirror. Then he braced the box so Todd could have a turn. Todd bashed and flabbered at the board.

"He's got such an innocent face," said Rick. "Does he get aggravated a lot? He's been pushing down on all these buttons and nothing's happening."

Todd gave the board one last bash and burst into tears. Rick abandoned the busy box and gathered him into his lap. "Let's leave this bad place," he said, "and go look out of the window instead."

Michael and Seth were trying to get up a game of catch with Freddy.

"Look, Freddy, a big boulder. Take it! Take it!" said Michael.

Freddy curled his hand away and hid it against his stomach.

"Shall I force him to hold it?" asked Michael.

"No. Suggest it," advised Seth. "Toss it up and down. Throw it to me. Look happy. Get him interested."

"We need the applemobile over here," Luke called across the room to Dylan.

"No. We're using it."

"I only need it for a second."

"We're using it," repeated Dylan. "We're just waiting for Brooke to get up her courage." He urged the mobile a little closer to Brooke and smiled enticingly.

"I think she hates it," Smith whispered.

"It's the scary eyes. I hated Mickey Mouse," said Dylan.

"You did? Me too."

"I was afraid of him. I was such a fool."

"Okay. Forget it," said Smith. "You give this apple thing to Luke and I'll go get the jack-in-the-box for her."

Smith returned with Forrest and Joey. Joey clutched the jack-in-the-box.

"It's my turn to turn," he said.

There was a commotion at the other end of the room. "He threw it! He threw it." Michael cheered and slapped his thigh.

"Good old Freddy. We should have lots of balls. I don't care what anyone says. Balls are best."

Seth patted Freddy on the shoulder.

"My favorite toy was a stuffed animal," said Luke, parking the applemobile between Freddy and Andrew. "I had this stuffed dog. He was bigger than I was. He used to hang around me all day. Want this panda, Andrew? I'll put a diaper on him for you."

Andrew paid no attention to him. He was busy experimenting with a wooden cylinder and the holes in the lid of Freddy's puzzle box. The cylinder dropped through the round hole with a clunk. Andrew looked around for another shape.

"Here. How about this one?" suggested Luke, holding out a cube. "You like this one?"

"Give him a hint where it goes," said Michael.

"Hey, you're right over it. Right over it. Drop it! Now! That's it. Crud. Well, here. Try again."

Andrew opened the top of the box, threw in the cube, and shut the top with a bang.

"I think he's a genius," said Luke, riding off on the mobile.

Brooke had lost interest in the jack-in-the-box. Her lower lip jutted out and her mouth turned down.

"She's going to cry again," said Smith. "Get more toys. Entertain her."

"We're trying," said Joey.

"Maybe it's her diapers," Forrest said.

"Move over guys. I'll get her," said Luke. He climbed off the big apple cart. "Lie her down."

"I'm trying," said Joey, "but I think she hates me. All she wants to do is sit up."

"She must be impossible to put to bed," said Forrest. "She did a job. I told you," he went on, checking her diaper. "Boy, did she do a job."

"I think this is the first time a baby's done both here," said Joey.

"Get the washcloth and the wipes and some paper towels. One wet and one dry one," said Luke.

"Oh, Brooke. You're amazingly cute. You're the cutest when you're crying," said Forrest.

"There. Done. Diapers, tabs, sweatsuit, everything. A record," said Luke. "Now, let's see a big smile. Say cheese."

"Hey, someone. We need the wipes," called Michael. "For Freddy."

"Why?" asked Seth. "He didn't even wet."

"I like changing."

"Who's going to wipe his nose? That's what he really needs."

"Not me. Yuck. No way."

"Boys, before we start cleaning up, see if you can answer this one," said Mrs. Maher. "What do you think is the best toy — the absolute best — for a baby?"

"A rag doll?"

"Something creative?"

"A ball," said Michael. "Definitely a ball."

"All good. But not the best," said Mrs. Maher.

"I've just blanked out," said Joey. His mouth wilted and his eyes rolled up.

"Look at Smith playing peek-a-boo with Brooke," hinted Mrs. Maher. "What kind of a toy is he using?"

"He isn't using anything," Gordon said.

"Hands?" said Rick.

"I know. Himself! Another person," said Seth.

"Yeah. Me. You. A friend. That's super!" said Luke.

"Sisters?"

"Sometimes," said Forrest.

"I wish my mother would have a baby. That would be best."

"Hey, Joey. Has your mother had your baby yet?" asked Seth.

"No. But it's gotta be any day now. It's already late, and my mother's parka is stretched to the limit."

"I hope it's a boy."

"I hope it's a girl."

"I don't care. I just want to be still in this class when it's born," said Rick.

89

The Sixth Wednesday

I'm going to be nice to my children. Every father wants to add something of his own experience. I'd encourage a good education, but if they wanted to give up in one subject, like English for example . . . if they thought they knew their stuff, I'd let them watch TV.

— *Smith*

I'm probably more capable at baby-sitting than a girl is. No offense. Girls get hysterical. They fidget. When things go wrong they don't know what to do. I get irritated when the babies cry, but you just keep whispering and patting and playing and eventually they stop.

— *Seth*

The only thing that makes you a good baby-sitter whether you're a girl or a boy is if you can stand them.

— *Rick*

When I grow up and have kids, I'm going to help my wife, because I want to and I should. When the baby's crying it isn't always hers and when it's laughing, it isn't always mine.

— *Douglas*

I've always loved babies. I think they're the smallest most cutest things you can have.

— *Luke*

HEY, JOEY, have you told her yet?" Luke leaned back on his hands, but he kept an eye on Andrew, who prowled around Caroline. Andrew had his eye on Caroline's toy toaster that popped up toy toast. Nearby, Smith was teaching Emily some basic calisthenics. On the other big mat Michael was trying to show Todd how to sit up straight, using Freddy as an example.

Joey beamed up at Mrs. Maher from under the visor of his baseball cap. "I've got a baby brother," he said.

"Wonderful, Joey!" said Mrs. Maher. "That's really terrific news! Have you seen him yet?"

"Yeah. He and my mom came home last night. I got to hold him, too. He's all red and wrinkled, and his legs are as long as his arms."

"Is your mom going to bring him in today?" asked Forrest.

"Well, no. My mom didn't remember he'd be so small. But she's *definitely* bringing him in next term."

"Next term? Oh, no! Hey, Mrs. uh . . . Mrs. . . . Caroline's mother? This isn't the last class, is it?" asked Forrest.

"Yes," said Mrs. Maher. "I'm afraid so."

"Are we going to get our certificates today?" asked Gordon and Rick at the same time.

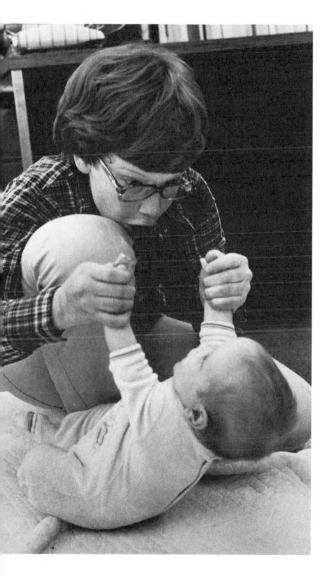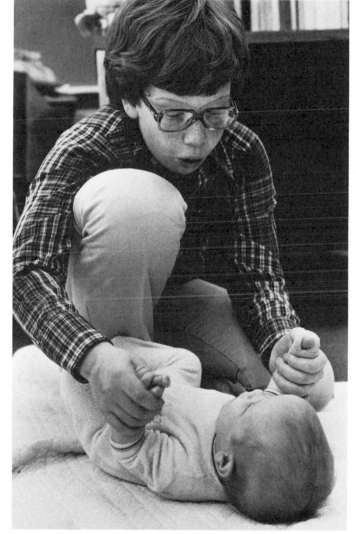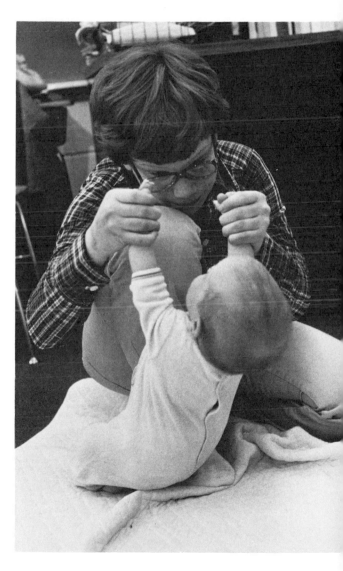

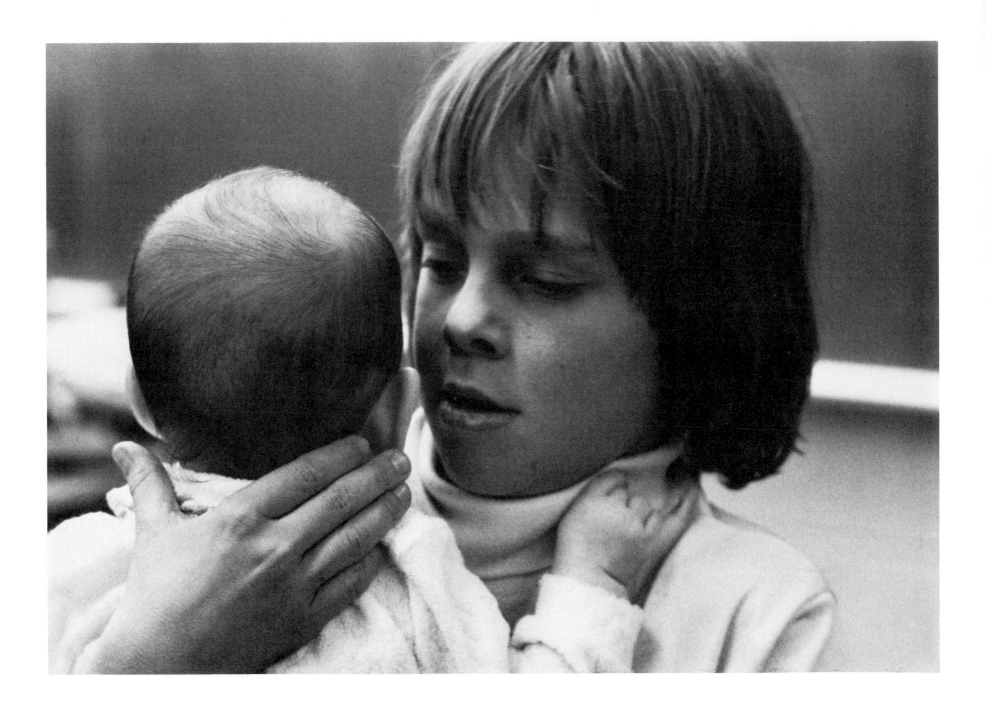

"I'm going to start baby-sitting as soon as I get mine," said Luke. "I'm tired of walking dogs."

"Did everyone, you know, pass?" asked Joey. Mrs. Maher didn't seem to hear him. She was busy at the sink unloading paper cups, bottles of soda, and tinfoil packages from two brown bags.

"I hope I fail. I hope I don't get my certificate," Dylan whispered to Henry. "I hope I have to repeat. That would be fun."

"I've got to get mine," said Joey. "To show my mom. Forrest, do you think Mrs. . . . ah, Mrs. Ma . . . counts for trying? Nothing really bad has happened since that time Brooke fell on her head."

"What's the 7-Up for?" asked Luke. "Are we having a party?"

"What's with all the questions?" countered Mrs. Maher, attempting to conceal the 7-Up behind the empty grocery bags. "At the moment the only thing we're having is a class, and you've got to be really with it today. You've got to take care of five babies, listen to me, and think, all at the same time."

"Think? About what?" asked Rick in a muffled voice. He was taking off Freddy's sneakers.

"About hazards and precautions," answered Mrs. Maher, moving to the middle of the room. "And more about the importance of questions, what to ask when you go baby-sitting. Before the parents leave you should find out where they can be reached, the name and telephone number of their pediatrician, and the names and numbers of friends or neighbors who could help if you had a problem."

"What about the poison-control number?" asked Gordon.

"Police? Fire?" added Smith.

"Turn on channel six. They have all the numbers," said Douglas.

"Only if you have cable," said Seth.

"You can find all those emergency numbers listed on the inside front cover of the telephone book. Okay? You should also check out front and back doors and emergency exits," said Mrs. Maher.

"Closets too. That's fun," said Forrest.

"Now. The parents have their coats on and they're half out the door," said Mrs. Maher. "What else do you need to know?"

"Things about the baby?"

"Special instructions," said Seth.

"What time she goes to bed? Does she have an allergy?"

"When the parents will be back?"

"And whether there's only health food in the refrigerator," said Luke under his breath. "If so, I'm not baby-sitting."

"Exactly," said Mrs. Maher. "And one more thing. Find out whether the parents are expecting any visitors while they're gone. If not, you answer the phone, of course, and take messages, but you don't open the door to anyone."

"Not even if it's Uncle Fester," said Rick.

"All right," Mrs. Maher went on. "Let's say the parents have left. You're on your own. What are some hazards you have to guard against?"

Forrest lay on his side without moving, watching Caroline

clamber up his back and down his front like a small bulldozer. Todd slowly listed toward the mat. "Babies are so loose," observed Michael, straightening him up again.

"Electrical plugs," said Luke without looking at Mrs. Maher. He took the toy toaster away from Andrew and gave it back to Caroline. "You gotta make sure they've put those little stopper things over them. Watch out, Seth. Watch out. Andrew's coming. Now he's after Freddy's bottle."

"Things on the floor that they can pick up and put in their mouths," said Rick.

"My cat cats dust balls," said Forrest.

"If they pull over a lamp, they could start a fire."

"Pins."

"Paper clips. Staples."

"Little trays with poisonous plants on them."

"Ropes. You shouldn't leave ropes around."

"Cigarette butts."

"Well, they could, you know," said Joey, "be sort of . . . or anything could happen."

"My mother said I used to pick used gum off the ground," said Rick.

"Match tips," said Forrest.

"Match tips?"

"Yes. I loved them. I still do. They're delicious."

"Right. All those things and more," said Mrs. Maher. "Crawlers and toddlers can find trouble anywhere. With infants your major concern is that they will roll over unexpectedly and fall off things. But for older babies, there is potential danger in every room. Take the kitchen, for example. . . ."

"Open windows."

"Window guards are good," said Seth. "I had those."

"They could turn the gas on in the stove," suggested Gordon.

"Or pull down pots of boiling water on their heads," said Douglas.

"Good thinking," said Mrs. Maher. "If you have to cook, keep the pots on the back burners or, at the very least, keep their handles turned in."

"Wet floors. They're slippery," said Rick.

"That's another good one," agreed Mrs. Maher. "If it's not too cold, I think bare feet are healthier and safer. They can grip the floor better whether it's wet or not."

"I knew it," said Rick. "I hate to walk around in clunky shoes, and I figure babies hate it too."

"You've got to watch out for the dryer," said Joey. "It's hot and gloomy in there."

"What about under the kitchen sink?" asked Mrs. Maher.

"Oh. Right. Floor waxes."

"Sprays."

"Pills. They think they're candy."

"Detergents."

"Deodorants," said Forrest.

"You should keep them high up so they can't get them," said Dylan.

"They can get anything. They can climb," said Joey. "I had

a cousin once who climbed into a cabinet. It was no bigger than a drawer. They found her, but only finally."

"Face it," said Seth. "The deal is you have to watch little kids all the time."

"You've got it," said Mrs. Maher. "That's it in a nutshell. Time to break out the 7-Up."

There were cheers and clapping.

"A party?" asked Luke. "What's there to eat?"

"Double trouble. Homemade brownies stuffed with chocolate chips," said Mrs. Maher. "And donuts and some other stuff. It's hidden behind the bags. Don't forget to offer some to the mothers."

"The certificates? What about them? Do we get them today?" asked Gordon.

"What certificates?"

"The diploma. The paper that says we've worked hard and deserve to get better," said Forrest. "The paper that says we're qualified."

Mrs. Maher bent her head and rummaged through her shoulder bag. "Ah ha," she said, pulling a manila envelope out of a side pocket. "This looks promising." Inside the envelope was a sheaf of papers. Rick tried to sneak a look at them, but Mrs. Maher held them close to her chest. "Documents," she said. "Definitely what we're after. The first one has your name on it, Seth. Congratulations." She handed him the certificate and shook his hand. Douglas was next and then Rick. "You did really well," she said. "Luke? Luke?"

"Just a sec. I've got to get this wad of Kleenex out of Caroline's mouth. Open your mouth, silly girl. Slobber. Slobber. Oh, gross, drool. You know what I mean? You feel a little wetness."

"Odel, odel, odel, odel, odel," said Caroline.

"Listen. She's learned to yodel," said Luke.

"That's nothing," said Smith. "Andrew can say 'queen,' 'kiss,' 'let,' and 'nine.' I'm sure I heard 'nine.' Or 'mime.' "

"Try Ricky." Rick put his face close to Andrew's and mouthed at him. "Ricky. Ricky. Ricky. Try Nicky. Maybe that's easier. Nicky. Nicky. Nicky."

Mrs. Maher put Luke's certificate to one side and shook hands with Michael and Gordon. Joey brushed the hair off his forehead and realigned his baseball cap. The visor was down to his eyebrows.

Luke was still dealing with Caroline so Mrs. Maher looked to see whose certificate was next. Just at that moment she was interrupted by a woman who pushed through the crowd of onlookers in the doorway and crossed the room to whisper in her ear.

"Boys . . . boys," Mrs. Maher raised a hand. "We've got a request. Does anyone want to baby-sit? After school?"

Almost all the boys raised their hands and some of them waved certificates.

"Okay. Let me see. All right, Seth. I saw your hand first. You're on. In the basement, the teacher's lounge, at 3:15. Now, who was I up to? Luke, are you ready?"

"Yes. Hey, Rick, watch Caroline for me."

Caroline grabbed the leg of a chair and tried to pull herself up.

"Hold on. Hold on! You're tilting," said Rick. "Yes! She stands! By herself. I've got to stick with her now."

"Can I take her for a walk?" asked Seth.

"No. She's mine, all mine. Go get your own baby."

Seth picked up a brownie for himself and a bottle of juice for Todd.

"I wonder how much that woman will pay me," Seth said between bites. "If she offers me a dollar, I can say, 'No, I've taken this course.' I can say, 'I get a dollar-fifty.' "

"Then she'll just go hire someone else," said Rick.

"Then I'll take the dollar."

"I'd even do it for free," Rick said.

Mrs. Maher shook hands with Luke. Joey put his hands in his pockets. There were only a few certificates left. Mrs. Maher congratulated Forrest, Smith, and Dylan. Joey strolled over to the sink and helped himself to a brownie and some 7-Up.

"Joey? Joey? Where are you?" called Mrs. Maher. "You were right here a minute ago. Don't tell me he's left without his certificate."

Joey dropped his brownie. He hurried back across the room wiping the crumbs off his mouth with the back of his hand. Then he wiped his hand on his pants before he held it out to Mrs. Maher.

"You learned a lot, Joey," said Mrs. Maher. "You're going to have a ball with your new baby brother."

Joey read his typed certificate. His name appeared twice, penned in by a calligrapher, and Mrs. Maher had signed her full name at the bottom, right above an official seal. The seal was dazzlingly red with serrated edges and embossed with the school's motto and crest. Joey ran his fingers over the raised surface. "How are we supposed to carry this thing around with us?" he asked Luke.

"Fold it, you fool," said Luke.

"I don't want to," said Joey. "I'm going to get it framed."

The brownies and donuts were disappearing fast, and the 7-Up was all gone. The only thing left to drink was a bottle of unsweetened natural apricot juice.

"Who brought this stuff in?" Douglas wanted to know. He helped himself to another brownie.

"These look like the best brownies I've ever tasted," said the boy from "Walls."

"Hey! Get your greasy fingers out of there! This is our party," said Luke. "There aren't even enough for the mothers."

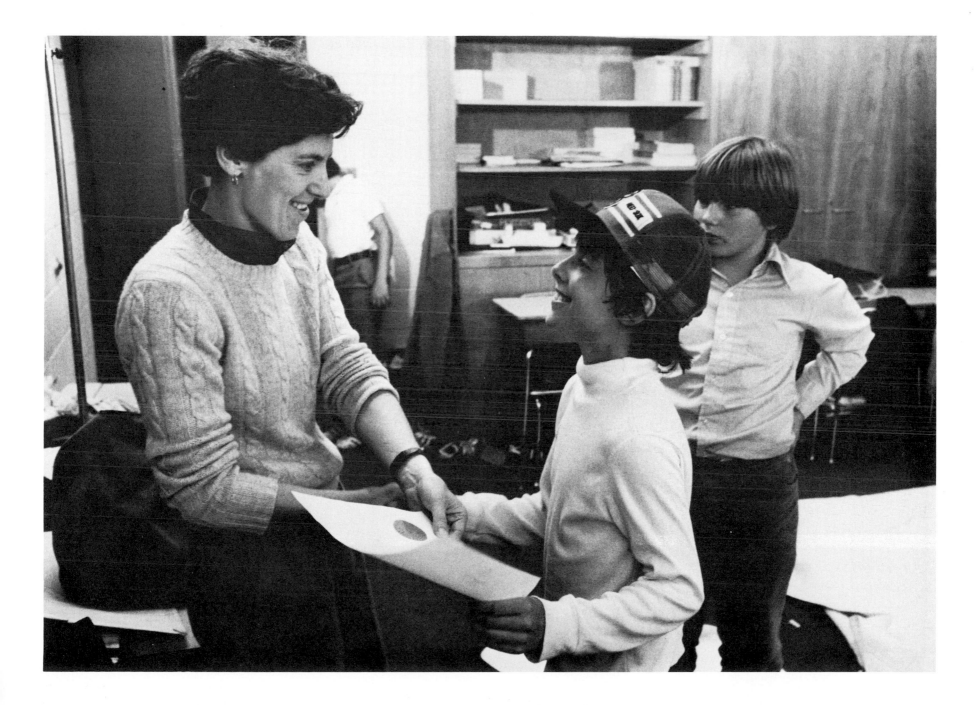

The boy from "Walls" put the brownie back, minus a bite. "I've signed up for this course next term," he said. "I put it first and third. Can I have an animal cracker?"

"They're for the babies," Luke told him.

"What am I going to give Andrew, besides this apricot juice?" Seth asked Mrs. Maher. "These cookies have sugar in them. I read the label."

Mrs. Maher produced some raisins in a plastic sandwich bag and Seth held one out to Andrew. Andrew took the raisin and ran. Seth followed him out the door and into the hall.

"I want to give Freddy one more stroll," said Luke. "Down to the water fountain and back. He likes to investigate. Where's his hot rod?"

On the way out Luke and Freddy passed Seth and Andrew coming in. Seth walked backward, luring Andrew with raisins.

"It was amazing," said Seth. "He charged right into Mr. Jacob's office. I've seen a lot of people wanting to get out of there but no one ever wanting to get in before."

Andrew's diaper sagged.

"We could try and change him," Joey said to Smith. "Want to risk it? What've we got to lose?"

"Sure. I'm game. First we've got to catch him."

"Right," said Joey. "Go for it."

The bell clanged in the hallway. "I'm afraid it's time, boys," said Mrs. Maher.

Gordon carried Emily over to where her mother was standing. "I'll zip her into the front pack for you," he said. "I know where her legs go and everything."

"I don't want this class to end," said Forrest. "I want to change Todd one last time. Quick. Where's a diaper?"

Michael was trying to fold up one of the big mats single-handedly, but Caroline thought it was a game.

"Caroline, if you'll just let go so I can finish this, I'll show you something," said Michael.

Forrest handed over Todd, freshly diapered and dressed, and Luke relinquished the stroller to Freddy's mother. "I'm sorry, Fred," he said. "Your animal cracker broke into three parts."

"Thank you, mothers," said Gordon.

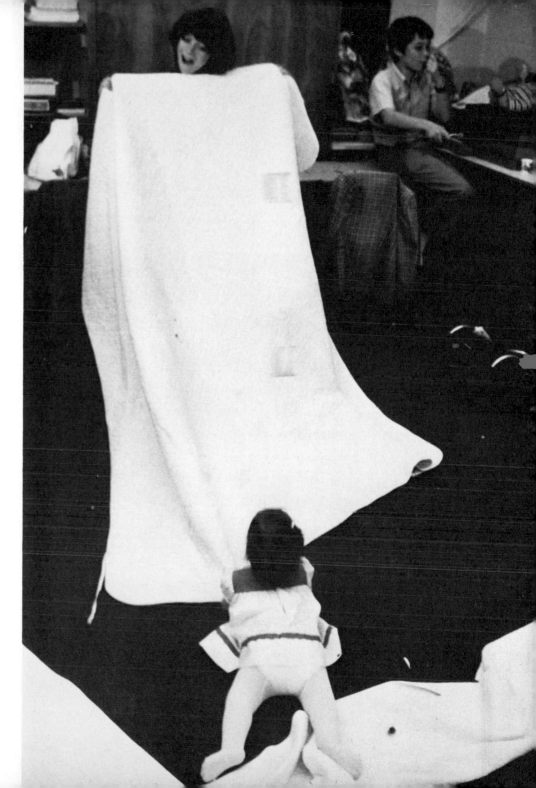

"Yes," said Luke. "Thank you. And thank you, Mrs. Mahurst."

Todd and Freddy were gone. Andrew's mother trailed Andrew out the door. Only Caroline and Emily were left.

Luke gave Emily a last hug.

Michael sat on the floor with Caroline and showed her the seal of his certificate. Mrs. Maher picked up Caroline's bottle and the last of her toys. Boys began to push the desks back into rows. Forrest watched the space around Michael and Caroline shrink.

"I'm going to beg and beg them to let me take the class again," Forrest said. "I'm going to sign up again even if I have to get down on my knees. I just love babies. I mean, I'm going to get down on my knees and beg them."

Afterword

EVEN THOUGH the class was expanded to twelve boys, Forrest did not get to repeat in the winter term. Too many other boys put "Babies" high on their list of alternatives. Next to "Computers" it was the most popular elective. However, more often than not, boys from the original ten dropped in on the class to say hello to Caroline and the others, to check out Joey's baby brother, and to offer advice and criticism.

Forrest did not sign up for "Babies" in the spring. He decided to wait out one term in hopes that Mr. Jacob would forget that he had taken the course before. His strategy worked. The following fall, when he listed the infant care class again, he got it and was able to hold, diaper, bathe, and feed a brand new batch of babies.